Test Your Rock IQ

The '70s

Also by Ira Robbins

The Trouser Press Record Guide
The Rolling Stone Review 1985
Test Your Rock IQ: The '60s

Test Your Rock IQ
The '70s

250 Mindbenders from Rock's Lost Decade

Ira Robbins

Illustrations by Kevin Markowski

Little, Brown and Company
Boston - New York - Toronto - London

First Edition

Library of Congress Cataloging-in-Publication Data

Robbins, Ira A.
Test your rock IQ: the '70s: disco and funk, metal and punk, 250 mindbenders from rock's lost decade / Ira Robbins: illustrations by Kevin Markowski. – 1st ed.
p. cm.
ISBN 0-316-74907-9
1. Rock music – 1971-1980 – Miscellanea. I. Title. II. Title: '70s.
ML3534.R56 1993
781.66'09–dc20 93-4414

10 9 8 7 6 5 4 3 2 1

Book design by Martha Kennedy

RRD-VA

Published simultaneously in Canada by Little, Brown & Company (Canada) Limited

Printed in the United States of America

Acknowledgments

Thanks to everyone who helped: my editor and friend Michael Pietsch for conceiving this project and for getting me between the covers (bookwise) in the first place; Wayne King, Dave Schulps, Jim Green, and Scott Schinder for their scholarship, fact-fixing, and invaluable criticism; Kevin Markowski for his wit, artistry, and deadline-beating delivery. And Mom and Dad and Bobo for the usual mushy stuff.

Ira Robbins
New York City

Test Your Rock IQ

The '70s

Introduction

The old joke about Woodstock—if you remember it, you weren't there—may also apply to the 1970s. These days, the decade when rock lost its innocence and ran into some stiff competition seems innocuous, a cheesy space in time when junk and big business were the only rulers in the pop jungle. At the merest mention of the '70s now, what springs to mind? Images of John Travolta in a white suit, finger pointing at Mars. Long-forgotten songs about citizens band radio. John Denver doing his granola shtick in a field somewhere. The Osmonds. Yeuch!

While mediocrity did rule, there were bright spots beyond the so-bad-it-now-sounds-good kitsch of disco and dreck, Grand Funk Railroad and the Captain and Tennille. Sure, the records that filled the airwaves by mid-decade were pretty awful, but they did inspire the new wave rebellion, so that's something. And if aging '60s legends had become unreliable sources of great music, at least some of them—like the Stones and the ex-Beatles and the Who and Dylan and Fleetwood Mac—did come across with the goods. Glam rock was a good laugh, and art rock wasn't always horrible. (Roxy Music saved the decade for me.) A few singer/songwriters actually had something to say and penned a few good tunes.

On second thought . . . Hopefully, these '70s musical brainteasers will bring a smile to your lips and a tap to your toe. If you haven't intentionally wiped from your memory everything you ever knew about this period, you may be surprised at how much you recall. How deep is your love? Take these five quizzes and find out.

SCORING

There are five quizzes of increasing difficulty in this book. Each quiz contains 50 questions. The answers have points indicated, so if you want to grade your expertise or challenge your friends to a rock trivia showdown, number a sheet of paper 1 to 50 and write down your answers. At the end of the quiz, compare your answers to those in the answer section at the back of the book and tote up your score. A perfect score for each quiz is 500.

In the interests of a chronologically level playing field, younger players should be given a quiz handicap—say, 10 points per year born after 1970. After all, it's a lot easier to remember this stuff if you lived through it.

Ratings

After you finish all five quizzes, if you've kept score, add up your total points for the entire book and see where you place on this '70s rock IQ scale:

under 500:	Just what were you doing in the '70s?
500–1000:	Back to schooldays
1001–1500:	Stuck in the middle
1501–2000:	You've got the music in you
2001–2500:	A wizard, a true star

Quiz 1:

Gabba Gabba Hey!

Well, this first quiz isn't that simple, but it does provide multiple-choice and matching sections to get you started on the road to the college of musical knowledge. All you need is a working knowledge of the names, dates, places, albums, and songs of '70s rock superstars, and you'll breeze through this one.

NAME THAT BAND

1. This popular duo came into being by accident, when an ex-member of Poco was hired to produce a rising young songwriter's first solo album.

    (a) Simon and Garfunkel
    (b) Seals and Crofts
    (c) Ferrante and Teicher
    (d) Hall and Oates
    (e) Loggins and Messina

2. Cattle, buffalo, and cactus were part of this group's onstage entourage for the 1976 Worldwide Texas Tour.

    (a) Johnny Winter And
    (b) Roky Erickson and the Aliens
    (c) ZZ Top
    (d) Butthole Surfers
    (e) Stevie Ray Vaughan and Double Trouble

3. Besides shifting more product than any other hard-rock group of the early 1970s, these guys bested the Beatles' box-office record by selling out two nights at Shea Stadium.

    (a) Aerosmith
    (b) Grand Funk Railroad
    (c) Mountain
    (d) Led Zeppelin
    (e) Rolling Stones

4. The lead singer of this raunchy Southern boogie band took his stage name from an old R&B song that the band covered. One of their albums contained a deed conferring ownership of a small plot—one square inch to be exact—of land in the band's home state.

    (a) Allman Brothers Band

(b) Marshall Tucker Band
(c) Lynyrd Skynyrd
(d) Black Oak Arkansas
(e) Outlaws

5. Years before the Sex Pistols launched their assault on the world, this American quintet shocked audiences by dressing in drag, vomiting in airports, and losing their first drummer to a drug-related drowning.

(a) Sic F*cks
(b) New York Dolls
(c) Iggy and the Stooges
(d) Alice Cooper
(e) Aerosmith

WHO ARE WE?

6. Tony Kaye, Rick Wakeman, Patrick Moraz, and Geoff Downes all played keyboards in this art-rock group, whose first album featured songs originally done by the Beatles and the Byrds.

(a) King Crimson
(b) Yes
(c) Emerson, Lake and Palmer
(d) Moody Blues
(e) Buggles

7. This funk overlord began building his empire as a singer in a '50s doo-wop group; by the mid-'70s, he was the central figure in a sprawling brigade of interrelated groups responsible for such dance anthems as "One Nation Under a Groove" and "Tear the Roof off the Sucker."

(a) Barry White
(b) James Brown
(c) George Clinton

(d) Rick James
(e) Sly Stone

8. In 1971, this British glam-rocker was forced to retitle the single that was about to bring his band international fame when an American group called Chase charted with a song by the same name.

(a) David Bowie
(b) Marc Bolan
(c) Alvin Stardust
(d) Gary Glitter
(e) Noddy Holder

9. Originally discovered by Kiss bassist Gene Simmons, this California quartet bears the surname of its guitarist and drummer.

(a) Angel
(b) Montrose
(c) Dokken
(d) Van Halen
(e) Giuffria

10. The first record by this British trio—who bleached their hair for a chewing gum commercial—was a 1978 song about a prostitute.

(a) Jam
(b) Police
(c) Hammersmith Gorillas
(d) Cure
(e) Fast

WHO IS ME?

11. Match the songs and the singers.

(a) "Me and Mrs. Jones" Janis Joplin

(b) "Me and You and a Dog Named Boo"	J. Geils Band
(c) "Me and Bobby McGee"	Lobo
(d) "Me and Julio Down by the Schoolyard"	Steve Miller Band
(e) "Me and Baby Brother"	Joni Mitchell
(f) "Me and My Arrow"	Nilsson
(g) "Give It to Me"	Orleans
(h) "Rock'n Me"	Billy Paul
(i) "Help Me"	Paul Simon
(j) "Dance with Me"	War

FRESHMAN ROCK HISTORY

12. Who performed his last concert on June 26, 1977, in Indianapolis?

(a) Elvis Presley
(b) Marc Bolan
(c) Sid Vicious
(d) Alice Cooper
(e) Brian Jones

13. Although surveys of FM radio listeners frequently identify it as the most requested rock song of all time, this 1971 album track has never been commercially released as a single. What number do they keep calling for?

(a) "Layla"
(b) "Won't Get Fooled Again"
(c) "Stairway to Heaven"
(d) "In-A-Gadda-Da-Vida"
(e) "American Pie"

14. The first 45 from this band's 1979 multi-platinum debut—an album reportedly recorded in 11 days for a total studio budget of $18,000—reached number one and set off the skinny-tie power-pop fad. By 1982, they were has-beens.

(a) Loverboy

(b) Boston
(c) Pilot
(d) Knack
(e) A Flock of Seagulls

15. All four members of what group released solo albums in October 1978?

(a) Who
(b) Led Zeppelin
(c) Television Personalities
(d) Yes
(e) Kiss

16. Who was the original Sex Pistols bassist before Sid Vicious?

(a) Tory Crimes
(b) Johnny Rotten
(c) Paul Simon
(d) Glen Matlock
(e) Tom Peterson

SOPHOMORE ROCK HISTORY

17. In July 1973, a British rock group doing a three-show stand at Madison Square Garden was relieved of $180,000 in ticket receipts from the vault of their New York hotel. Who was the victim of this robbery?

(a) Rolling Stones
(b) Who
(c) Jethro Tull
(d) Led Zeppelin
(e) Deep Purple

18. What band managed the amazing feat of getting a four-disc live album to the number three spot in Billboard in 1971?

(a) Grand Funk Railroad
(b) Chicago
(c) Jackson 5
(d) Canned Heat
(e) Grateful Dead

19. What pop performer bought the publishing rights to Buddy Holly's songs in the mid-1970s and instigated an annual Buddy Holly Week celebration in England?

(a) Elton John
(b) Paul McCartney
(c) Dave Clark
(d) Michael Jackson
(e) Screaming Lord Sutch

20. On a 1977 Christmas TV special, David Bowie crooned a surprisingly sweet duet of "Peace on Earth" and "Little Drummer Boy" with the show's star. Who was Bowie's vocal partner?

(a) Stevie Wonder
(b) Dolly Parton
(c) Dean Martin
(d) Bing Crosby
(e) Frank Sidebottom

21. Which rock 'n' roll star climbed over the fence of Graceland in the middle of an April 1976 night only to be nabbed by a security guard?

(a) Bruce Springsteen
(b) Jerry Lee Lewis
(c) Carl Perkins
(d) Madonna
(e) Little Richard

SINGERS AND RINGERS

Which member of each band is (or was) its lead vocalist?

22. Roxy Music

(a) Phil Manzanera
(b) Brian Eno
(c) Andy Mackay
(d) Bryan Ferry
(e) Sal Maida

23. Mott the Hoople

(a) Ian Hunter
(b) Mick Ralphs
(c) Overend Watts
(d) Mick Ronson
(e) Dale Griffin

24. Ramones

(a) Joey Ramone
(b) Marky Ramone
(c) Johnny Ramone
(d) Tommy Ramone
(e) Richie Ramone

25. Boston

(a) Tom Scholz
(b) Brad Delp
(c) Barry Goudreau
(d) Sib Hashian
(e) Fran Sheehan

26. Deep Purple

(a) Glenn Hughes
(b) Ian Gillan
(c) Roger Glover
(d) Tommy Bolin
(e) Jon Lord

ODD MEN OUT

Each of these quintets includes a musician who's never been in a band with the other four. For each lineup, pick out the ringer and name the group .

27. (a) Tony Banks
(b) Peter Gabriel
(c) Steve Hackett
(d) Steve Howe
(e) Mike Rutherford

28. (a) Tom Hamilton
(b) Joey Kramer
(c) David Johansen
(d) Steven Tyler
(e) Brad Whitford

29. (a) Ritchie Blackmore
(b) Geezer Butler
(c) Ozzy Osbourne
(d) Tony Iommi
(e) Bill Ward

30. (a) Syd Barrett
(b) David Gilmour

(c) Nick Mason
(d) Rick Wright
(e) Robert Wyatt

31. (a) Denny Doherty
(b) Joe English
(c) Denny Laine
(d) Jimmy McCullough
(e) Denny Seiwell

FAINT PRAISE AND DUBIOUS CLAIMS

32. Which British quartet was dubbed "the only English group that matters" in the '70s?

(a) Clash
(b) Led Zeppelin
(c) Who
(d) Kinks
(e) Steely Dan

33. Who has been called, among other dubious sobriquets, "the world's most elegantly wasted human being" and "the human riff"?

(a) Johnny Thunders
(b) Keith Richards
(c) Jerry Lee Lewis
(d) Nick Kent
(e) Chuck Berry

34. What nonexistent band—which nonetheless released an album and was the subject of a one-hour television profile in 1978—billed itself as "The Prefab Four"?

(a) Kiss
(b) Archies

(c) Monkees
(d) Rutles
(e) Spinal Tap

35. What singer/songwriter was accused of bigotry for his ironic 1977 putdown of "Short People"?

(a) Paul Williams
(b) Paul Simon
(c) Randy Newman
(d) Jackson Browne
(e) Bob Dylan

36. Which American guitarist of the '70s, who claimed to have been visited by the spirit of Jimi Hendrix, based a career on his ability to mimic Hendrix's style?

(a) Frank Marino
(b) Robin Trower
(c) Stevie Ray Vaughan
(d) Jimmy Buffett
(e) Alan Douglas

37. Match the musician with his or her onetime nickname:

(a) Bruce Springsteen	Bonzo
(b) Clarence Clemons	Thin White Duke
(c) David Bowie	Buffin
(d) Jerry Garcia	Night Tripper
(e) John Bonham	Pearl
(f) Nick Lowe	Plonk
(g) Dr. John	Captain Trips
(h) Janis Joplin	Boss
(i) Dale Griffin	Basher
(j) Ronnie Lane	Big Man

ALBUMS YOU PROBABLY OWN

Using this list of 20 possible answers, pick out which classic '70s album contains each of the song trios in questions 38 through 42.

(a) David Bowie, The Rise and Fall of Ziggy Stardust and the Spiders from Mars
(b) Clash, The Clash
(c) Cheap Trick, In Color
(d) Doors, Morrison Hotel
(e) Doors, L. A. Woman
(f) Michael Jackson, Off the Wall
(g) John Lennon, Imagine
(h) Pink Floyd, The Dark Side of the Moon
(i) Rolling Stones, Goat's Head Soup
(j) Rolling Stones, Exile on Main Street
(k) Roxy Music, For Your Pleasure
(l) Todd Rundgren, Something/Anything?
(m) Simon and Garfunkel, Bridge Over Troubled Water
(n) Bruce Springsteen, Darkness on the Edge of Town
(o) Talking Heads, Fear of Music
(p) T. Rex, The Slider
(q) T. Rex, Electric Warrior
(r) Who, Quadrophenia
(s) Stevie Wonder, Talking Book
(t) Neil Young, After the Gold Rush

38. "Love Her Madly," "The WASP (Texas Radio and the Big Beat)," "Riders on the Storm"

39. "Southern Girls," "Clock Strikes Ten," "Hello There"

40. "Rock with You," "She's Out of My Life," "Don't Stop 'Til You Get Enough"

41. "I'm So Bored with the U.S.A.," "Career Opportunities," "Garageland"

42. "Rip This Joint," "All Down the Line," "Happy"

DATES

43. In which years (between 1970 and 1979) were the following albums released?

(a) Bruce Springsteen, Born to Run; Patti Smith, Horses; Neil Young, Tonight's the Night; Bob Dylan, Blood on the Tracks; Peter Frampton, Frampton Comes Alive

(b) Derek and the Dominos, Layla and Other Assorted Love Songs; John Lennon/Plastic Ono Band; Van Morrison, Moondance; Captain Beefheart, Trout Mask Replica; Traffic, John Barleycorn Must Die

(c) Who's Next; Marvin Gaye, What's Going On; Alice Cooper, Killer; Cat Stevens, Tea for the Tillerman; Rolling Stones, Sticky Fingers

(d) Saturday Night Fever; Sex Pistols, Never Mind the Bollocks; David Bowie, Heroes; Wire, Pink Flag; Fleetwood Mac, Rumours

(e) New York Dolls; Wings, Band on the Run; Pink Floyd, The Dark Side of the Moon; Iggy and the Stooges, Raw Power; Lou Reed, Berlin

44. In which years (between 1970 and 1979) were the following singles hits?

(a) "Rock the Boat," Hues Corporation; "Bennie and the Jets," Elton John; "Band on the Run," Wings; "It's Only Rock and Roll (But I Like It)," Rolling Stones

(b) "Heart of Glass," Blondie; "Pop Muzik," M; "Is She Really Going Out with Him?" Joe Jackson; "My Life," Billy Joel

(c) "Let It Be," Beatles; "Tears of a Clown," Miracles; "Teach Your Children," Crosby, Stills, Nash and Young; "Lola," Kinks

(d) "School's Out," Alice Cooper; "Join Together," Who; "Long Cool Woman (In a Black Dress)," Hollies; "Take It Easy," Eagles

(e) "Love Is the Drug," Roxy Music; "Beth," Kiss; "Boogie Fever," Sylvers; "Let Your Love Flow," Bellamy Brothers

45. In the Temptations' 1972 chart-topper "Papa Was a Rolling Stone," what makes the 3rd of September a day to remember?

UNDER THE COVERS

46. Who came first? The original may be the greatest, but it's not always the one people remember. With that in mind, which artist listed after each classic song did it first?

(a) "Brother Louie"
Stories
Hot Chocolate

(b) "Take Me to the River"
Al Green
Talking Heads

(c) "Never Can Say Goodbye"
Gloria Gaynor
Isaac Hayes
Jackson 5

(d) "Hooked on a Feeling"
Jonathan King
B. J. Thomas
Blue Swede

(e) "Proud Mary"
Creedence Clearwater Revival
Ike and Tina Turner

ROCKING ALL OVER THE WORLD

47. Great Britain and America may provide the majority of the world's internationally prominent rock 'n' roll bands. But not all of them. Match up these bands with their nationality: American, British, Australian, or Canadian.

(a) Ace

(b) Rick Springfield
(c) Styx
(d) Eric Burdon
(e) Steely Dan
(f) Neil Young
(g) Klaatu
(h) Average White Band
(i) Mungo Jerry
(j) Nick Gilder

48. From this list of 10 places, match the song titles and the geographical names missing from them:

Boston	Rome	Tokyo
California	San Diego	East L.A.
Chicago	San Francisco	Texas
Denver		

(a) "Woman from ______________" (Deep Purple, 1973)
(b) "The Night ______________ Died" (Paper Lace, 1974)
(c) "Get Out of ______________" (Bob Seger, 1974)
(d) "Please Come to ______________" (Dave Loggins, 1974)
(e) "Hotel ______________" (Eagles, 1977)

49. With no list to choose from, fill in the geographical names missing from these song titles:

(a) "______________ Freedom" (Elton John, 1975)
(b) "______________ Grove" (Doobie Brothers, 1973)
(c) "______________ Queen" (Mountain, 1970)
(d) "______________ Rock City" (Kiss, 1976)
(e) "______________" (Crosby, Stills, Nash and Young, 1970)

50. In which city is Deep Purple's autobiographical "Smoke on the Water" set?

(a) Marseilles

(b) Memphis
(c) Milan
(d) Montreal
(e) Montreux

Quiz 2:
Take It Easy

More questions about bands and records. This quiz also has multiple choices and matching sections, but the topics are ever so slightly harder, requiring a deeper awareness of the decade's musical landmarks and leading personalities, including Rod Stewart and Bruce Springsteen. And get that glitter ball lit up to see what you can remember about the disco era.

PAST LIVES

51. Since the beginning of the 1970s, as a member of both the Faces and the Rolling Stones, Ron Wood has been known strictly as a guitarist. For a spell in the '60s, however, he was a bassist. In what band?

(a) Artwoods
(b) Jeff Beck Group
(c) Creation
(d) Small Faces
(e) Birds

52. In 1972, John Lennon engaged an underground New York band to back him and Yoko Ono live and in the studio. The group appeared on the couple's Some Time in New York City and Live in New York City, as well as Ono's Approximately Infinite Universe. Who was this chosen ensemble?

(a) Fugs
(b) David Peel and the Lower East Side
(c) Death of Samantha
(d) Fly Ashtray
(e) Elephant's Memory

53. Leon Russell became a major star in the '70s, landing gold awards for a half-dozen solo albums. In the '60s, however, he was a top L. A. sessionman, tinkling the ivories for Phil Spector, the Byrds, Herb Alpert, and others. He also did arrangements, scoring a bunch of hits with one particular group. Who?

(a) Gary Puckett and the Union Gap
(b) Tommy James and the Shondells
(c) Dwight Twilley
(d) Gary Lewis and the Playboys
(e) Grass Roots

54. In the late 1960s, before his solo career took off, Rick James fronted a long-forgotten Toronto band called the Mynah Birds. Another alumnus of that group would also move south of the border and become a star. Who?

(a) Neil Young
(b) Joni Mitchell
(c) Burton Cummings
(d) Bryan Adams
(e) Gordon Lightfoot

55. David Robinson of the Cars and Jerry Harrison of Talking Heads both cut their teeth in a legendary band from Boston, a group whose first album, recorded as demos for an aborted label deal in 1971, was released five years later. Who?

(a) Willie Alexander and the Boom Boom Band
(b) Lyres
(c) Modern Lovers
(d) Real Kids
(e) Barry and the Remains

COVERS

56. Which two members of Fleetwood Mac appear on the front cover of Rumours?

(a) Mick Fleetwood and John McVie
(b) John McVie and Christine McVie
(c) Stevie Nicks and Lindsey Buckingham
(d) Mick Fleetwood and Stevie Nicks
(e) John McVie and Stevie Nicks

57. Which London landmark is pictured on the cover of Pink Floyd's Animals?

(a) Battersea Power Station
(b) Trafalgar Square
(c) Big Ben
(d) Westminster Abbey
(e) Buckingham Palace

58. The front cover of Get Yer Ya-Ya's Out! features a bemused-looking pack mule and a member of the Rolling Stones. Which one?

(a) Mick Jagger
(b) Keith Richards
(c) Bill Wyman
(d) Charlie Watts
(e) Mick Taylor

59. What article of clothing was included in original copies of Alice Cooper's School's Out?

(a) tie
(b) underpants
(c) sock
(d) hat
(e) handkerchief

60. Which member of the Clash appears on the front cover of London Calling?

(a) Joe Strummer
(b) Mick Jones
(c) Terry Chimes
(d) Topper Headon
(e) Paul Simonon

61. What species of animal shares the front cover of Tapestry with Carole King?

(a) dog
(b) cat
(c) horse
(d) elephant
(e) parrot

IS IT LIVE?

Pick out the concert recording from each of these veterans' 1970–1980 albums.

62. Van Morrison

(a) A Period of Transition
(b) His Band and Street Choir
(c) Into the Music
(d) It's Too Late to Stop Now
(e) Moondance

63. Grateful Dead

(a) At the Mars Hotel
(b) Grateful Dead
(c) Shakedown Street
(d) Wake of the Flood
(e) Workingman's Dead

64. Lou Reed

(a) Growing Up in Public
(b) Lou Reed
(c) Metal Machine Music
(d) Rock n Roll Animal
(e) Street Hassle

65. Neil Young

(a) Comes a Time
(b) Everybody Knows This Is Nowhere
(c) Time Fades Away
(d) Rust Never Sleeps
(e) Tonight's the Night

66. Bob Marley and the Wailers

(a) Babylon by Bus
(b) Burnin'
(c) Catch a Fire
(d) Exodus
(e) Uprising

MOONLIGHTING

67. In 1980, Linda Ronstadt took a break from rock and pop by singing and acting onstage in a work by Gilbert and Sullivan. In which operetta did she perform?

(a) H.M.S. Pinafore
(b) The Mikado
(c) The Gondoliers
(d) The Pirates of Penzance
(e) Iolanthe

68. Which member of the Rolling Stones was the first to release a solo record?

(a) Mick Jagger
(b) Keith Richards
(c) Bill Wyman
(d) Charlie Watts
(e) Brian Jones

69. Robert Fripp, onetime leader of King Crimson, now operates a school in West Virginia. What does this institution teach?

(a) accounting
(b) computer programming
(c) synthesizer design
(d) guitar playing
(e) band management

70. Who can often be heard preaching at the Full Gospel Tabernacle church in Memphis, Tennessee?

(a) Donny Osmond
(b) Little Richard
(c) Bobby Richardson
(d) Jerry Lee Lewis
(e) Al Green

71. What baseball legend added play-by-play to a million-selling album released in 1977?

(a) Bob Uecker
(b) Phil Rizzuto
(c) Mel Allen
(d) Tom Seaver
(e) Reggie Jackson

72. The titular subject, co-writer, and guest star of Led Zeppelin's "Boogie with Stu" (1975) was an adjunct member of another British supergroup. Who was Stu?

(a) Rod Stewart
(b) Al Stewart
(c) Ian Stewart
(d) Stewart Copeland
(e) Stuart Moxham

MOONLIGHTING IN PAIRS

73. Which two singers made guest appearances on Alice Cooper's Billion Dollar Babies and Muscle of Love albums?

(a) Screaming Lord Sutch
(b) Liza Minnelli
(c) Ray Davies
(d) Donovan

(e) George Burns
(f) Gordon Lightfoot

74. Which two of these artists have had albums produced or co-produced by David Bowie?

(a) Iggy Pop
(b) Warren Zevon
(c) Nile Rodgers
(d) Patti Smith
(e) Ric Ocasek
(f) Lou Reed

75. Which two of these performers were lucky enough not to appear in Robert Stigwood's 1978 film Sgt. Pepper's Lonely Hearts Club Band?

(a) Aerosmith
(b) Ringo Starr
(c) Peter Frampton
(d) Michael Jackson
(e) Wilson Pickett
(f) Tina Turner

NAMES

76. What 1985 British supergroup had almost the same name—albeit in a different language—as a pioneering European techno band who had an American hit in 1975?

(a) Band Aid
(b) Power Station
(c) Incredible String Band
(d) Man
(e) Can

77. Which U.K. teenybop band got most of its name from a map of Michigan?

(a) Neu
(b) MC5
(c) McGuinness Flint
(d) Detroit Spinners
(e) Bay City Rollers

78. Which Charles Dickens character provided the name for a Washington, D.C., band of the mid-'70s?

(a) Mister Macawber
(b) Artful Dodger
(c) Fagin
(d) Uriah Heep
(e) David Copperfield

79. Exactly how is the title of Led Zeppelin's "Dyermaker" punctuated on Houses of the Holy?

(a) "Dyer Maker"
(b) "D'yer Maker"
(c) "Dyer Ma'ker"
(d) "D'yer Mak'er"
(e) "Dy'er M'aker"

80. Stage names, please:

(a) Vincent Furnier
(b) Reginald Dwight
(c) Declan Patrick MacManus
(d) Gene Klein
(e) Marvin Lee Aday
(f) John Mellor
(g) Yvette Marie Stevens
(h) Stuart Goddard
(i) Peter Blankfield

(j) Mark Feld

THE MANY FACES OF ROD STEWART

81. Throughout the early '70s, Rod Stewart juggled his role as lead singer in the Faces with a solo career, alternating releases and scoring hits with both. But with that distinctive voice and a related cast of supporting musicians, who can remember which 45s were solo Rod and which also featured the Faces?

(a) "Cindy Incidentally"
(b) "Maggie May"
(c) "Reason to Believe"
(d) "Stay with Me"
(e) "You Wear It Well"

82. On the same topic, which of these albums were by the Faces and which were Stewart solo efforts?

(a) Gasoline Alley
(b) Every Picture Tells a Story
(c) A Nod's as Good as a Wink . . . to a Blind Horse
(d) Never a Dull Moment
(e) Ooh La La

83. Although personally responsible for writing his share of great tunes, Rod Stewart is also a connoisseur of covers. Match up the Stewart recording with an artist who did it first.

(a) "Only a Hobo"	Jimi Hendrix
(b) "Cut Across Shorty"	Elton John
(c) "My Way of Giving"	Sam Cooke
(d) "Country Comforts"	Bob Dylan
(e) "(I Know) I'm Losing You"	Maxine Brown

(f) "Reason to Believe" Tim Hardin
(g) "Angel" Eddie Cochran
(h) "Twistin' the Night Away" Chris Farlowe
(i) "Oh! No Not My Baby" Etta James
(j) "I'd Rather Go Blind" Temptations

NOVELTEASE

84. Despite a long and productive career, contained on such albums as Attempted Mustache, T Shirt, and Final Exam, this singer/songwriter/actor (M*A*S*H) is widely known for only one song, a silly 1973 ditty about road kill. Name him.

(a) Loudon Wainwright III
(b) Kinky Friedman
(c) John Prine
(d) Peter Stampfel
(e) Arlo Guthrie

85. One of the strangest hits of 1971 was a recitation by TV talk-show host Les Crane of a poem written in 1906 under the title "Go Placidly Amid the Noise and Haste." Crane's record (savaged on the National Lampoon's Radio Dinner LP) bore a different name. What was it?

(a) "Catch It You Keep It"
(b) "Love Is Blue"
(c) "An Open Letter to My Teenage Son"
(d) "Desiderata"
(e) "Take It Easy"

86. Dickie Goodman made a big splash in 1975 with a cut-in record based on a blockbuster horror film released earlier that year. Name the movie.

(a) Nightmare on Elm Street
(b) Friday the 13th
(c) Halloween

(d) The Shining
(e) Jaws

87. After spending eight years away from the Top 40, Chuck Berry returned to the charts in 1972 with a risqué million-seller recorded live in England. Name that tune.

(a) "My Ding-a-Ling"
(b) "Brown Eyed Handsome Man"
(c) "Havana Moon"
(d) "Chuck's Berries"
(e) "Nadine"

88. What group's 1972 debut album had an abundantly fragrant cover?

(a) Rhinoceros
(b) Elephant's Memory
(c) Rubber City Rebels
(d) Raspberries
(e) Mom's Apple Pie

BRUCE SPRINGSTEEN

89. Two national magazines ran cover stories on Bruce Springsteen the same week in October 1975. Which pair?

(a) Time and Life
(b) TV Guide and Newsweek
(c) Newsweek and Time
(d) Billboard and TV Guide
(e) Rolling Stone and Time

90. What up-from-the-underground New York rocker hit it big in 1978 with a song Springsteen co-wrote?

(a) Debbie Harry

(b) Patti Smith
(c) Lou Reed
(d) Richard Hell
(e) Elliot Murphy

91. Which Springsteen album yielded no official American singles?

(a) Greetings from Asbury Park, N.J.
(b) Born to Run
(c) Darkness on the Edge of Town
(d) The River
(e) The Wild, the Innocent & the E Street Shuffle

92. In 1977, who got the first number one hit with a Bruce Springsteen song?

(a) Bruce Springsteen
(b) Pointer Sisters
(c) Manfred Mann's Earth Band
(d) Air Supply
(e) Hollies

93. Which of the following bands never included Bruce Springsteen in its lineup?

(a) Castiles
(b) Steel Mill
(c) Southside Johnny and the Asbury Jukes
(d) Dr. Zoom and the Sonic Boom
(e) Child

ROCK AND ROLL AND ROCK AND ROLL

94. The subject of rock 'n' roll itself has proven to be an irresistible lyrical idea for far too many bands. Overlooking several songs simply named "Rock and Roll," match these not too imaginatively titled tunes to the groups that dreamed them up.

(a) "Rock and Roll Part 2" Bad Company

(b) "Rock and Roll All Nite" Bay City Rollers
(c) "Rock and Roll, Hoochie Koo" Blue Öyster Cult
(d) "Rock'n'Roll Love Letter" David Bowie
(e) "Rock & Roll Soul" Eric Carmen
(f) "Rock 'n Roll with Me" Rick Derringer
(g) "Rock 'n' Roll Fantasy" Gary Glitter
(h) "A Rock 'N' Roll Fantasy" Grand Funk Railroad
(i) "Cities on Flame with Rock and Roll" Kinks
(j) "That's Rock 'n Roll" Kiss

THE DISCO BEAT

95. With hits as a solo act, as an orchestra leader, and as the Svengali of a vocal group, this singer/writer/producer sold a reported $16 million worth of records in 1973. Who is he?

(a) Prince
(b) Barry White
(c) Rick James
(d) Arthur Baker
(e) Marvin Gaye

96. Which character was not in the original Village People?

(a) policeman
(b) native American
(c) biker
(d) cowboy
(e) football player

97. Who's the Memphis disc jockey that had a 1976 hit with the novelty single "Disco Duck (Part I)"?

(a) Rick Dees
(b) Dr. Demento

(c) Steve Dahl
(d) Dewey Phillips
(e) Casey Kasem

98. In 1976, an up-tempo dance arrangement of a classical classic took Walter Murphy to the top of the charts. What composition did he borrow?

(a) Beethoven's Fifth
(b) Ravel's Bolero
(c) Debussy's Prélude à l'Après-midi d'un Faune
(d) Beethoven's Eroica
(e) Wagner's Ride of the Valkyries

99. Besides producing dance hits for Donna Summer and others, Giorgio Moroder has successfully composed soundtrack music. For which 1978 film did he win an Academy Award?

(a) American Gigolo
(b) Don't Stop the Music
(c) Midnight Express
(d) Carwash
(e) Sgt. Pepper's Lonely Hearts Club Band

100a. While living in England, American singer Amii Stewart remade a Stax soul classic with a disco beat and had an international chart-topper in 1979. What song did she cover?

(a) "Can't Turn You Loose"
(b) "Knock on Wood"
(c) "Walking the Dog"
(d) "My Guy"
(e) "Y.M.C.A."

b. Which artist did the song originally?

(a) Temptations
(b) Sam and Dave
(c) Eddie Floyd
(d) Rufus Thomas
(e) Village People

Rock 'n' Roll Quiz 3: High School

Nobody said this would get easier. With no multiple-choice suggestions, you'll need to come up with the answers to these next 50 brainbusters on your own. So dig back into the memory banks and see how well you recall the soft-rock sounds of California, the hard-rock sounds of the Who, and such cultural ephemera as commercial jingles, posthumous successes, and great songwriters of the '70s.

CALIFORNIA SINGING

101. Whose wistful love song about California threatened to "kiss a Sunset pig"?

102. Albert Hammond was never able to repeat the success of his 1972 soft-rock smash "It Never Rains in Southern California." But two years later, he borrowed another bit from nature and co-wrote a huge hit for the Hollies. Name the song.

103a. Shortly after being drafted by Linda Ronstadt to be part of her backing band in 1971, a group of musicians declared themselves the Eagles and launched a monumentally successful career. Who were the original Eagles?

b. Which of them was the first to quit the group?

c. On what album did guitarist Joe Walsh become an Eagle?

104. Neil Young's American Stars 'n Bars album (1977) featured backup vocals by Linda Ronstadt and a singer who also worked on his next release. Identify her and the song that became her first solo hit in 1978.

105. After spending the '60s in a British Invasion duo with Gordon Waller, Peter Asher became a significant force in American music as the production guru behind Linda Ronstadt's and James Taylor's best-selling records. One artist for whom Asher supervised a 1979 album went on to a much bigger career without him. Name that singer/guitarist.

106. Which of these singer/songwriters, all of whom helped define the sound of Southern California in the '70s, were actually born in the state?

(a) Joan Baez
(b) Jackson Browne
(c) Albert Hammond
(d) Kenny Loggins
(e) Joni Mitchell
(f) Graham Nash
(g) Linda Ronstadt
(h) Stephen Stills
(i) James Taylor
(j) Warren Zevon

FAMILY AFFAIRS

107. All but one of these bands contains (or contained) siblings. Which one never has? AC/DC, Bachman-Turner Overdrive, Beach Boys, Bee Gees, B-52's, Heart, Kinks, Ramones, Sparks, Spring, Styx

108. Name the group led in the '70s by bassist Jean Millington and her guitar-playing sister, June.

109. A 1974 solo album by Mike McGear, veteran of the humorous English groups Scaffold and Grimms, was co-written and produced by his more famous big brother. Name him.

110. Sweet Baby James wasn't the only Taylor to launch a recording career in the '70s. Which of his siblings also made albums that decade?

111. Before launching a band of his own in 1970, this saxophone-playing keyboardist served as a sideman in his brother's group. Who?

112. A year after Michael Jackson's first solo hit, one of his siblings also successfully stepped into the spotlight. Which 18-year-old Jackson remade Shep and the Limelites' "Daddy's Home" for a 1972 smash?

113. No points for knowing how many Jacksons were in the Jackson 5. But what about the Osmond family?

(a) How many performing Osmonds were there?
(b) How many of them—besides Donny and Marie—can you name?

BAD IDEAS AND ASSORTED BOONDOGGLES

114. Which group claimed to have mixed their own blood in with the red ink used to print a comic book about them?

115. In one of the most ill-conceived promotional concepts ever, an Irish band's American record label sent radio stations dead animals sealed in plastic bags. What group's career was supposed to be aided by this bright idea?

116. In 1977, a North American group that would not reveal the identities of its members became the center of media speculation that it was, in fact, the Beatles recording under a pseudonym. What was the name of this mystery group?

117a. Which British rock star announced that he was retiring from live performance at the finish of a 1973 London concert?

b. In what year did his next tour take place?

118. The 1976 Grammy Award for Best New Artist went to a one-hit wonder on the strength of a coy song about midday sex. The following year, a singer best known for having a famous daddy repeated the flash-in-the-pan Best New Artist feat with a sappy movie ballad. From this sorry list of candidates, pick the two lucky winners.

(a) Paper Lace
(b) Starland Vocal Band
(c) A Taste of Honey
(d) Silver
(e) Wild Cherry
(f) Vicki Lawrence
(g) Maureen McGovern
(h) Vicki Sue Robinson
(i) Natalie Cole
(j) Debby Boone

RECIPES FOR CONSTRUCTION

119. In 1970, three members of a long-running British blues band broke away and formed a new group that had far greater American success than its predecessor ever would. Name both bands.

120. In its original incarnation, Bad Company was comprised of refugees from what three groups?

121. Former members of the Nice, King Crimson, and Atomic Rooster provided the lineup for what enormously successful 1970s trio, a rock band that did not include a full-time guitarist?

122. From which British Invasion group did the namesake of the group that did "Hold Your Head Up" in 1972 hail?

123. Although they came to prominence amid the new wave youth movement, the Police were not exactly new kids on the rock block.

(a) Name the British progressive rock ensemble in which Stewart Copeland played prior to the Police.
(b) Name any two of Andy Summers's pre-Police bands.

COMMERCIALS

124. What 1972 Carly Simon song was used to sell ketchup?

125. For what product did Lou Reed allow "Walk on the Wild Side" to be used as a jingle?

126. What Jim Webb song—a 1967 hit for an American vocal group—became a TWA jingle?

127. Which soda jingle, adapted from a song entitled "True Love and Apple Pie," was covered for hit singles by two different groups—one British, one American—in 1971?

POSTHUMOUS SUCCESS

128. This cigar-smoking singer/songwriter had his first number one single three months before the September 1973 airplane crash that killed him. By the end of the year, another one of his songs had reached the top of the charts. Who was he?

129. AC/DC's fame and fortune grew by leaps and bounds after the 1980 demise of singer Bon Scott. When a 1976 Australian LP featuring him was finally issued in the U.S. five years after the fact, it sold a million-plus copies. What was the album?

130. Three days after its 1977 release, an album by this group was withdrawn when a plane crash killed its lead singer, a guitarist, and a backup singer. The untimely cover photo, which pictured the septet standing in flames, was altered and the record rereleased. Name the band and the album.

THE WHO

131. Despite their enormous popularity, the Who never had a number one album in America. Two of their albums (both released in the '70s), however, made it to the penultimate position. Which ones?

132. Name the three songs not written by Pete Townshend that are included on Live at Leeds.

133. Who drew the cover of The Who by Numbers?

134. What is the protagonist of Quadrophenia called?

135a. What was the title of Keith Moon's 1975 solo album?

b. What was the name of the band with whom John Entwistle undertook an American solo tour in 1975?

c. One half of the songwriting team Roger Daltrey used for his first solo album became a singing star in his own right. Who?

d. Which song on Who's Next is sung entirely by Pete Townshend?

CAN I BORROW A SONG?

136. None of these songs were written by members of the bands that made them into hits. They were, however, all composed by famous singers. Identify the performers who wrote these songs they didn't popularize:

(a) "All the Young Dudes" Mott the Hoople
(b) "Woodstock" Crosby, Stills, Nash and Young
(c) "Stir It Up" Johnny Nash
(d) "Mama Told Me (Not to Come)" Three Dog Night
(e) "The City of New Orleans" Arlo Guthrie

137. What song did the courts decide George Harrison had "unknowingly" plagiarized for the melody of "My Sweet Lord"?

138. Which hard-rocking Californians made a splashy debut in 1978 with a souped-up version of a British Invasion rock classic?

139. Although this group emerged from the New York punk underground, its first success came in England with a sex-change remake of a 1963 hit by Randy and the Rainbows.

(a) Who was the group?
(b) What was the song's original title?

140. This Scottish band—which had already turned songs by Joni Mitchell, Bob Dylan, and Woody Guthrie into loud, dramatic rock—made the American Top 40 in 1976 with an Everly Brothers cover.

(a) What band was it?
(b) What song did they do?

MORE SONG BUSINESS

141. More than a decade before Mötley Crüe revived "Smokin' in the Boys Room," the original was a huge hit for a Michigan trio. Name the group.

142. For which Paul Simon song did Aretha Franklin win a 1971 Grammy for Best Rhythm and Blues Vocal Performance (Female)?

143. "It's Too Late," songwriter Carole King's first million-seller as a performer, came out the same year as her composition "You've Got a Friend" brought another singer/songwriter his first gold single. Name him.

144. What dance record's bass line provided the spine for the Sugarhill Gang's 1979 hip-hop groundbreaker, "Rapper's Delight," as well as the basis for a Queen hit the following year?

145. When an ex-Beatles helped a friend rerecord a tune he had sung with the Fab Four, their collaboration yielded a 1975 number one. Name the song.

PEOPLE WHO SING ABOUT PEOPLE

146a. Which song, written in response to a Neil Young record, mentions the singer/songwriter by name?

b. Which Neil Young song started this brouhaha?

c. In what song did Neil Young subsequently make an allusion to the whole business?

147. What real person is Pink Floyd's "Shine on You Crazy Diamond," from Wish You Were Here, about?

148. Barry Manilow and David Cassidy had the hits with it, but someone else actually composed "I Write the Songs" about the main songwriter in a band in which he plays.

(a) Who wrote it?
(b) Who is the song about?

149. The title (as well as the lyrics and music) of a 1977 chart-topper from Stevie Wonder's Songs in the Key of Life paid fond tribute to which American musical institution?

150. Match the songwriters with the real people whose names appear in their song titles:

(a) Bob Dylan	Pablo Picasso
(b) John Lennon	Wolfman Jack
(c) Brian Wilson	John Sinclair
(d) Ian Dury	Jackie Wilson
(e) David Bowie	Andy Warhol
(f) Jonathan Richman	Johnny Carson
(g) Alice Cooper	Marie Prévost
(h) Todd Rundgren	George Jackson
(i) Nick Lowe	Gene Vincent
(j) Van Morrison	Dwight Frye

Tough enough to separate the serious rock scholar from your garden-variety fan, this quiz checks out your knowledge and memory of such crucial '70s phenomena as glam rock, heavy metal, and new wave/punk, not to mention singles, record producers, rock on film, and song lyrics.

GLAM ROCK AND GLITTER

151. Match the opening-line lyrics with the glitter-rocker who recorded them. Then name the tunes.

(a) "Make me a deal and make it straight"
(b) "Zoo time is she and you time"
(c) "Well you're dirty and sweet"
(d) "Billy rapped all night about his suicide"
(e) "You've got your mother in a whirl"
(f) "Hey kid, rock'n'roll"
(g) "I don't want to drink my whiskey like you do"
(h) "You better beware, you better take care"
(i) "Look out, look out your momma will shout"
(j) "Standing in the corner at the dance last night"

Mott the Hoople
David Essex
Gary Glitter
David Bowie
Slade
Wizzard
Sweet
T. Rex
Sparks
Roxy Music

NAMESAKES

152. Which instrument did/do these musicians play in the groups that bore/bear their name? Your choices: guitar, bass, drums, keyboards.

(a) J. Geils of the J. Geils Band
(b) Larry Graham of Graham Central Station
(c) Harry Casey of K.C. and the Sunshine Band
(d) Brinsley Schwarz of Brinsley Schwarz
(e) Robert "Kool" Bell of Kool and the Gang
(f) Ronnie Montrose of Montrose

153. Which of them are or were the lead singers of their groups?

HEAVY METAL

154. Identify these heavy rock groups by their '70s drummers:

(a) Alan Moore
(b) Phil Taylor
(c) Ian Paice
(d) Rudy Lenners
(e) Phil Rudd
(f) Andy Parker
(g) Lee Kerslake
(h) Gil Moore
(i) Albert Bouchard
(j) Darrell Sweet

155. Name the monsters of rock responsible for these '70s albums, none of which, it must be noted, reached the American Top 40:

(a) Caress of Steel
(b) Some Enchanted Evening
(c) Sad Wings of Destiny
(d) Technical Ecstasy
(e) Fly to the Rainbow
(f) Long Live Rock'n'Roll
(g) Rock'n'Roll Machine
(h) Twin Peaks
(i) Mad Love
(j) Helluva Band

156. In the early '70s, guitarist Mike Pinera, late of Blues Image and Iron Butterfly, joined ex-Hendrix drummer Mitch Mitchell in an undistinguished heavy band called Ramatam, which debuted with an eponymous album in 1972. The group's sole claim to fame was that it featured a female guitarist. Name her.

THANKS, I'LL REMAKE IT MYSELF

157. What British singer took the liberty, on his 1976 Let's Stick Together solo album, of remaking five songs by his band?

158. What English group that evolved from another had a 1977 American hit by redoing a 1972 classic from the repertoire of its parent band?

159. Jimmy Page has never been one to let a good guitar pattern go to waste. Which two Led Zeppelin songs were adapted from the Yardbirds' "White Summer"?

160. What song was a Top 40 hit in two different versions – recorded a decade apart – by its author, Don McLean?

161. What song on the first Bad Company record did guitarist Mick Ralphs reprise from his tenure with his former band?

162. In 1979, a live version of a song that had flopped as a 1977 single became a gold-plated hit for this American band. Name the group and the song.

SURFING A NEW WAVE

163. When MTV went on the air in August 1981, the first song played was a prescient slice of 1979 new wave. Which song launched the video revolution?

164. The Ramones' second album, 1977's Leave Home, was withdrawn and reissued with one track deleted. What song was it?

165. Name the two pivotal punk bands Richard Hell co-founded but left before they made their debut albums.

166a. What American pop singer had the temerity to cover three Elvis Costello songs on one 1980 album?

b. Name those songs and another Costello composition the artist previously recorded.

167. Which British punk band was the first to release a full-length album and the first to tour the U.S.?

168. Name the first Clash album to be released in America.

169. The 1979 single that launched the 2 Tone label featured two different bands. The A-side contained the Specials' "Gangsters," while the flip was an instrumental credited to a group that didn't yet exist. Who was the phantom combo?

170a. What British independent record company founded in 1976 launched the career of Elvis Costello and many other important artists?

b. In 1978, the same label released a compilation album of bands (Waitresses, Bizarros, Rachel Sweet) from a midwestern American city. Name the city.

c. What delectable local aroma did the scratch 'n' sniff cover of that release release?

171. Match the pseudonymous musicians and their bands:

(a) Johnnie Fingers	Stranglers
(b) Steve Nieve	Dictators
(c) Rat Scabies	Boomtown Rats
(d) Billy Zoom	Germs

(e) Darby Crash — Dead Boys
(f) Poly Styrene — X
(g) Jet Black — Damned
(h) Lux Interior — X-Ray Spex
(i) Cheetah Chrome — Attractions
(j) Top Ten — Cramps

YOU MUST RE-MEMBER THIS

172. How many members of Fleetwood Mac, past or present, can you name?

173. Besides their solo and group work, David Crosby, Stephen Stills, Graham Nash, and Neil Young have collaborated on albums in various combinations. So far, they've tried only a fraction of the possible permutations. Which of these six duos have actually released albums?

(a) Crosby and Stills
(b) Crosby and Nash
(c) Crosby and Young
(d) Stills and Nash
(e) Stills and Young
(f) Nash and Young

174. Name the drummer who played in each of these trios of bands:

(a) Move, Electric Light Orchestra, Black Sabbath
(b) Vanilla Fudge, Cactus, Rod Stewart
(c) Jeff Beck Group, Mothers of Invention, Journey
(d) Yes, King Crimson, Genesis
(e) Dust, Richard Hell and the Voidoids, Ramones

175. Who were the other two original Wailers besides Bob Marley?

176. Going by the back cover of 1972's Holland album, the Beach Boys were a seven-man group at the time. Name all the members of this extended family.

PRODUCERS

177. Each of these odd couples of groups from the '60s and '70s have a producer in common. Name the studio veterans who worked on albums by:

(a) Vanilla Fudge and the New York Dolls
(b) Climax Blues Band and the Sex Pistols
(c) Tyrannosaurus Rex and Iggy Pop
(d) Billy J. Kramer & the Dakotas and Jeff Beck
(e) Free and the Clash

178. What groups (other than their own) or solo artists had albums produced in the '70s by these famous bassists?

(a) John Entwistle
(b) Bill Wyman
(c) Klaus Voorman
(d) Stanley Clarke
(e) Jack Casady

DEATH

179. Janis Joplin, Jimi Hendrix, and Alan Wilson died in 1970. Duane Allman, Gene Vincent, King Curtis, and Jim Morrison all died in 1971. Each of those below checked out in one of the years between 1972 and 1979. Supply the correct years:

(a) Sid Vicious
(b) Gram Parsons
(c) Phil Ochs
(d) Berry Oakley
(e) Keith Moon
(f) Mama Cass Elliott
(g) Tim Buckley
(h) Marc Bolan

INSTRUMENTALS

180. Two dissimilar instrumentals, coincidentally performed by men sharing the same initials, became million-sellers in 1973. One was used in a movie soundtrack, the other shared a title with a film classic. Enough clues? Name the two hits.

181. Only two years before taking home a Grammy for Best Male R&B Vocal Performance, he won a pair of Grammys for his instrumental work. Who?

182. Months after the LP's original release, an excerpt from this instrumental solo album became a hit single when it was used as the musical theme of a 1974 film. Identify the album and the movie.

THE MOVIES

183. In the 1974 film Stardust (the sequel to That'll Be the Day), Dave Edmunds led the fictional band that backs David Essex's character and appears on the soundtrack performing such rock 'n' roll classics as "When Will I Be Loved" and "Some Other Guy." Seven years later, Edmunds produced a real band by the same name. Who?

184. What name did screenwriters Roger Ebert and Russ Meyer give to the fictional all-female group in Meyer's 1970 skin-rock-violence-exploitation cult classic, Beyond the Valley of the Dolls?

185. The Saturday Night Fever soundtrack, released at the end of 1977, sold 25 million copies, spawned four number one singles and was named the 1978 Album of the Year at the Grammy awards. But who wrote the magazine article on which the film was based?

186. Name five movie scores written and performed in the '70s by Curtis Mayfield.

SINGLES CLUB

187. What Irish group's 1979 single, while not a major chart smash here, received loads of airplay, most often on a certain day of the week?

188a. Marvin Gaye's three consecutive smash singles in 1971 all came off one classic album. Name the LP.

b. Name the 45s.

189. Pink Floyd's Dark Side of the Moon, released in 1973, sold well in excess of 10 million copies and spent more than a decade on the charts. But it gave rise to only one hit single. Which song?

190. The producer of Grand Funk's first chart-topper, "We're an American Band," also scored the biggest hit of his solo career in 1973. Who was he and with what song was it?

191. Released in February 1977, Fleetwood Mac's Rumours became one of the biggest-selling albums of the decade. Four songs from it became Top 10 singles that year. Name them.

192. When Roger Daltrey stuttered the lyrics to "My Generation," he was suggesting the jitters mods got from taking speed. A decade later, and for entirely different reasons, a Canadian group stuttered its way to the top of the charts. Name the hit.

193. Don Henley sang lead on two of the three hit singles taken from Hotel California. Which Eagle sang the third, and which song was it?

194. After this American group's debut single topped the charts in 1979, the lyrics of the song picked as its follow-up had to be rewritten in order to censor the blatant vulgarity of the album track. Name the song.

SONG CHARACTERS, REAL AND IMAGINED

195. The Clash's "Jail Guitar Doors," the B-side of 1978's "Clash City Rockers," makes pointed reference to three guitarists who've had brushes with the law. Who are the song's subjects?

196. In "You're So Vain," Carly Simon observes that the song's subject is "where you should be all the time." But if not, who is he likely to be with?

197. With whose niece does the narrator of Bob Dylan's "When I Paint My Masterpiece" have a date?

198. Nils Lofgren's eponymous 1975 solo album contains his heartfelt tribute to a real-life rock star. Name the song.

199. Name the songs in which these characters appear and the artists who sang about them.

(a) Jungle Faced Jake

(b) Jack, Stan, Roy, Gus, and Lee
(c) Twig the Wonder Kid
(d) Spanish Johnny
(e) Tom, Robin, and Rick

200. Name five of the film stars who make cameo appearances in the Kinks' "Celluloid Heroes."

Quiz 5:

Block buster

Ready to give up? Nothing's easy about this final quiz, which runs the gamut from mushy Top 40 crud to the Sex Pistols, record labels to pseudonyms, song titles to chart failures. Admittedly no one needs to know any of this stuff, but bragging rights definitely go to anyone who can ace this examination of obscure alternatives.

HAVE A NICE DECADE

201. What 1974 novelty hit concerned a goofy fashion fad that reached its cultural climax on that year's Academy Awards telecast?

202. What sound effect on R. Dean Taylor's 1970 hit "Indiana Wants Me" caused an unexpected problem and was subsequently excised from radio station copies of the record?

203. One member of late-'60s pop flop Lewis and Clarke Expedition (named neither Lewis nor Clarke) scored in 1975 with a sappy song about a horse. He has since flourished as a country rocker. Who?

204. In 1970, four British groups had their first American hits: the Edison Lighthouse's "Love Grows (Where My Rosemary Goes)," White Plains' "My Baby Loves Lovin'," the Pipkins' "Gimme Dat Ding," and the Brotherhood of Man's "United We Stand." Other than their nationality and success, what do the four records have in common?

205. Besides a talented lineup of Scottish and English folk-rockers, Stealers Wheel boasted a venerable American songwriting/production team in its corner. Together, they made "Stuck in the Middle with You" a 1973 hit. Who were Stealers Wheel's two illustrious producers?

206. The 1978 *Wings Greatest* compilation contains a dozen Paul McCartney singles (including five chart-toppers) released between 1971 and 1978: "Another Day," "Silly Love Songs," "Live and Let Die," "Junior's Farm," "With a Little Luck," "Band on the Run," "Uncle Albert/Admiral Halsey," "Hi, Hi, Hi," "Let 'Em In," "My Love," "Jet," and "Mull of Kintyre." All well and good. But which 1975 number one single does the collection inexplicably omit?

FLIPSIDES

207. What hideously schmaltzy 1974 million-seller had as its B-side a piece of doggerel (later covered by Soul Asylum) entitled "Put the Bone In"?

208. Although it was also released as a one-side-long edit, which 1971 smash (total running time 8:32) took up both sides of a single?

209. In 1979, Nick Lowe rescued a song that he had co-written from a British B-side (where he had given it a disco arrangement) and recut it for Labour of Lust. When the new version was released as an A-side, Lowe squirmed his way to an American hit.

(a) What was the song?
(b) In what band did Lowe and co-writer Ian Gomm once play together?

210. Johnny Winter included a pair of Jagger/Richards compositions on his 1973 Still Alive and Well album. That same year, one of the songs—which had been written for Winter—also became a Rolling Stones B-side. Name the tune and the Stones hit it backed up.

SEX PISTOLS

211. During their brief existence, the Sex Pistols were signed to three different British labels. Two of those actually released records by the group, but only one provoked a Pistols song title. Name all three.

212. December 1, 1976: Appearing with some of their fans on a British TV talk show, the Sex Pistols are provoked into a rude tirade that caused a public furor ("The Filth and the Fury" was the most memorable tabloid headline) and nearly cancelled their Anarchy in the U.K. tour.

(a) Who hosted this televised debacle?

(b) What subsequently famous punk vocalist was part of the fan contingent that appeared with the group on the show?

213. In which cities did the Pistols begin and end their January 1978 American tour?

214. Name two Eddie Cochran songs recorded by the Sex Pistols.

STAGE DIVERSE

215. What 1974 album by a Major Rock Star consists entirely of between-song concert banter?

216. In January 1973, Pete Townshend, Ron Wood, Steve Winwood, Jim Capaldi, and others served as sidemen for a well-known musician's comeback concert, documented on a live album. Who was the evening's star?

217. Name any member of the band that backed Peter Frampton on the multimillion-selling Frampton Comes Alive! album.

218. What five songs did Bob Dylan perform at the Concert for Bangla Desh?

219. Nine bands—the cream of Britain's first safety-pin crop plus a cheesy European import—took the stage at the watershed 100 Club Punk Rock Festival, held in London on September 20 and 21, 1976. Who were they?

NAME THAT TUNESMITH

220. The songwriters are household names; these songs of theirs from the '70s may be a bit less familiar. Can you name the composer of each quartet of tunes?

(a) "Love Is Coming Down," "Mother and Son," "Misunderstood," "Too Much of Anything"

(b) "Talk to Me," "Janey Needs a Shooter," "If I Was the Priest," "Rendezvous"

(c) "A New Career in a New Town," "Candidate," "Right," "Word on a Wing"

(d) "Something There Is About You," "Golden Loom," "Sign Language," "Buckets of Rain"

(e) "Girlfriend," "Wonderful Christmastime," "Warm and Beautiful," "What Do We Really Know?"

221. After a decade of knocking around the country music business–sweeping up studios, road managing, serving as a sideman to Kris Kristofferson and Kinky Friedman, producing Tony Joe White–this Nashville cat made it to the top of the charts with an original tune later covered by Elvis Presley.

222. In the early '70s, an obscure singer/songwriter playing Los Angeles bars under a pseudonym wrote a number about the sorry state of his career. A year later, the song became the Top 40 title track from an LP that ultimately sold a million copies.

(a) Who is he?

(b) Under what name had he been performing?

(c) A song he wrote and recorded in tribute to a '60s girl group was subsequently covered by its original lead singer. Name the song and the vocalist.

223. Over the years, an assortment of artists have recorded albums in tribute to the work of others. Who devoted albums to these songwriters?

(a) Randy Newman

(b) Charles Mingus
(c) Buddy Holly
(d) Bob Dylan
(e) Lefty Frizzell

224. Although Elton John has co-written nearly all his hits with lyricist Bernie Taupin, he has had success with other collaborators.

(a) Name the lyricist who co-wrote the songs for 1978's A Single Man.
(b) Name two American hits (1976 and 1983) on which Elton and Taupin share songwriting credit with guitarist Davey Johnstone.
(c) Name an Elton John album on which he received no songwriting credit whatsoever.

FAR GONE AND OUT

225. Like the familiar story of Pete Best and the Beatles, many bands have ex-members who were there at the beginning but gone by the time major stardom came knocking. Name the bands these musicians bowed out of in the early innings.

(a) Gary Valentine
(b) Terry Chimes
(c) Harry Kakoulli
(d) Stephen Duffy
(e) Mick Abrahams

226. Each of these musicians left well-known bands to try greener pastures. Name the bands the following formed upon leaving the fold.

(a) Paul Kossoff, ex-Free
(b) Glenn Cornick, ex-Jethro Tull
(c) Ariel Bender, ex-Mott the Hoople

(d) Tony Kaye, ex-Yes
(e) Howard Devoto, ex-Buzzcocks

227. By the end of 1980, how many U.S. or U.K. solo albums (discounting compilations, soundtracks, group projects, and collaborations) had been released by the founding members of Roxy Music (Bryan Ferry, Brian Eno, Andy Mackay, and Phil Manzanera)?

A LABEL OF MY OWN

228. Identify the artists who owned (if not necessarily recorded for) these labels that opened for business in the '70s.

(a) Swan Song
(b) Rocket
(c) Konk
(d) Dark Horse
(e) Tuff Gong
(f) Manticore
(g) Grunt
(h) Hot Buttered Soul
(i) 2 Tone
(j) Unlimited Gold

NAMES AND TITLES

229. Since song titles can't be copyrighted, they can be—and occasionally are—applied to different compositions that otherwise have nothing in common. Each of these odd couples shared a song title in the '70s: you have to

figure out what it was. Warning: not all the songs were released as singles, nor were they all hits. For what it's worth, the answers are arranged alphabetically.

(a) Sweet and Aerosmith
(b) Todd Rundgren and the Raspberries
(c) Carole King and Derek and the Dominos
(d) Kiss and Marvin Gaye
(e) Damned and Anne Murray
(f) Neil Diamond and Roxy Music
(g) Cheap Trick and Geils
(h) Squeeze and Cheap Trick
(i) Black Sabbath and T. Rex
(j) Rick James and Queen

230. The following groups changed their names—some unwillingly—early in their careers. Who did they become?

(a) Halfnelson
(b) In Betweens
(c) Tiger Lily
(d) Earth
(e) Warsaw

231. Which well-known artists hid behind these pseudonyms?

(a) Blue Ridge Rangers
(b) Neil MacArthur
(c) Suzy and the Red Stripes
(d) Mutations
(e) Hank Wilson

PLAYERS CLUB

What do each of these groups of groups have in common?

232. The Band, 10cc, Eagles, Carpenters, Dwight Twilley Band

233. Runaways, League of Gentlemen, Talking Heads, Adverts

234. Lynyrd Skynyrd, Eagles, Black Oak Arkansas, Outlaws

235. Grateful Dead, Genesis, Allman Brothers Band, Doobie Brothers

236. Cars, Wings, Devo, Records, (English) Beat

WE BELONG TOGETHER

Some common denominator unifies each of these lists. What?

237. Patti Smith, Lenny Kaye, Bob Geldof, Chrissie Hynde, Neil Tennant

238. Pain, Pleasure, Ecstasy, Fire, Honey, Gold, Angel

239. Sweet, Mud, Suzi Quatro, Smokie

240. Night, street, ride, dark(ness), road

241. Graham Simpson, Sal Maida, John Wetton, Rick Wills, Gary Tibbs

242. Shoot Out at the Fantasy Factory (Traffic), Happy to Meet . . . Sorry to Part (Horslips), Odds & Sods (Who), Physical Graffiti (Led Zeppelin)

243. Mike Oldfield, Gong, Faust, Henry Cow, Link Wray

THOSE WACKY BRITS

244. All these albums reached the top chart spot in Great Britain during the 1970s, yet none made any major commercial impact on America at the time. Can you name the disappointed artists? (Labels and release dates are all U.K.)

(a) Atom Heart Mother (Harvest, 1970)
(b) Fog on the Tyne (Charisma, 1972)
(c) Stranded (Island, 1973)
(d) Old, New, Borrowed and Blue (Polydor, 1974)
(e) Hergest Ridge (Virgin, 1974)
(f) On the Level (Vertigo, 1975)
(g) Once Upon a Star (Bell, 1975)
(h) Stupidity (United Artists, 1976)
(i) Night Flight to Venus (Hansa/Atlantic, 1978)
(j) Replicas (Beggars Banquet, 1979)

LOOSE LIPS

245. About whom did Lester Bangs remark, in a 1977 article, "Here was I, a grown man, travelling all the way across the Atlantic Ocean . . . just to ask a goddamn rock 'n' roll band for the meaning of life!"

246. What artist used the slogan "Go ahead. Ignore me" in 1972 print ads for a two-disc solo album?

247. In what paper was Jon Landau's oft-quoted (and evidently self-fulfilling) May 1974 prophecy about Bruce Springsteen published?

248. As filmed in The Decline of Western Civilization, what San Francisco punk rocker coined the expression "Eat my fuck"?

249. To whom did Elvis Costello venture his infamous 1979 Ohio barroom slur about the race and vision of Ray Charles?

250. "Ever have the feeling you've been cheated?" Who wanted to know?

Answers

NAME THAT BAND

[10 POINTS PER CORRECT ANSWER]

1. (e) Loggins and Messina. A year after ex–Buffalo Springfield singer/guitarist Jim Messina exited Poco, he was hired to produce Kenny Loggins's solo album. They wound up collaborating on the record (released in 1972 as Kenny Loggins with Jim Messina Sittin' In), launching a partnership that lasted until 1976.

2. (c) ZZ Top. The trio's epochal road trip involved more than a hundred American dates and concert stops in Asia, Europe, and Australia.

3. (b) Grand Funk Railroad. In the summer of '72, the little ol' band from Flint, Michigan, demonstrated the enormity of its artistic achievements by selling out two nights at the New York Mets' palace in 48 hours.

4. (d) Black Oak Arkansas. A weird mixture of crude sexuality and old-time religion made washboard-toting Jim Dandy Mangrum and his triple-guitar boogie brothers a popular live attraction. In 1974, a cover of "Jim Dandy" (originally sung by LaVern Baker in the '50s) became BOA's only Top 40 single.

5. (b) New York Dolls. Although they had not yet recorded and were little known outside New York's nascent underground club scene, the Dolls were flown to England in late 1972 to open a show for the Faces at Wembley Arena. During the trip, drummer Billy Murcia drowned in a London bathtub.

WHO ARE WE?

[10 POINTS PER CORRECT ANSWER]

6. (b) Yes. Formed by veterans of various obscure groups–the Syn, Warriors, Mabel Greer's Toy Shop, and Bitter Sweet–Yes got a break in 1968, opening Cream's farewell concert. Yes, released the following year, contained six of the quintet's originals plus novel arrangements of the Byrds' "I See You" and the Beatles' "Every Little Thing."

7. (c) George Clinton. The Ohio native began his career in the '50s as lead singer of

the Parliaments, a vocal group that had a 1967 hit with the rocking "(I Wanna) Testify." In the '70s, he crossed psychedelia, humor, and heavy funk, creating a danceable solution with its own fanciful language and exotic characters. Funkadelic, Parliament, P. Funk, Brides of Funkenstein, Bootsy's Rubber Band, and others were all part of Clinton's mothership.

8.(b) Marc Bolan. "Get It On" was T. Rex's second British number one around the same time American jazz-rock group Chase (led by trumpeter Bill Chase, a genuine big-band veteran) had an unrelated record with the same title in the U.S. charts. For its subsequent American release, the T. Rex song was retitled "Bang a Gong (Get It On)."

9.(d) Van Halen. The two Van Halens—guitarist Eddie and drummer Alex—were born in Holland but raised in California, where they formed the group that bears their name in 1974. Gene Simmons produced a demo tape for the band in 1976; the quartet's debut album was released in 1978.

10. (b) Police. Sting, Andy Summers (who replaced Henry Padovani after one 1977 single), and Stewart Copeland began their hugely successful career together with the reggae-accented "Roxanne."

WHO IS ME?

[1 POINT PER CORRECT ANSWER]

11. (a) "Me and Mrs. Jones" Billy Paul
    (b) "Me and You and a Dog Named Boo" Lobo
    (c) "Me and Bobby McGee" Janis Joplin
    (d) "Me and Julio Down by the Schoolyard" Paul Simon
    (e) "Me and Baby Brother" War
    (f) "Me and My Arrow" Nilsson
    (g) "Give It to Me" J. Geils Band
    (h) "Rock'n Me" Steve Miller Band
    (i) "Help Me" Joni Mitchell
    (j) "Dance with Me" Orleans

FRESHMAN ROCK HISTORY

[10 POINTS PER CORRECT ANSWER]

12. (a) Elvis Presley. He died on August 16. Two months later, a live album (Elvis in Concert) recorded at two shows on that final Midwest tour was released.

13. (c) "Stairway to Heaven." While Led Zeppelin did issue some 45s in America –"Whole Lotta Love," "Immigrant Song," and others–the group never released a 7-inch "Stairway to Heaven." In England, there were no Zeppelin singles at all.

14. (d) Knack. "My Sharona" sold over 2 million copies in 1979, making the salacious Los Angeles quartet an overnight sensation. Get the Knack, produced by Blondie producer Mike Chapman, sold by the carload, but the group–which made two additional LPs, broke up, and then reformed for a postscript album in 1991–never equaled its success.

15. (e) Kiss. Gene Simmons, Paul Stanley, Ace Frehley, and Peter Criss all issued eponymous, cover-art-coordinated solo albums on the same day. The chart ranking: Simmons, Frehley, Stanley, and, bringing up the rear, drummer Criss. Guitarist Frehley even managed a hit single ("New York Groove") from his.

16. (d) Glen Matlock. Originally the group's main songwriter, Matlock was allegedly sacked for liking the Beatles. In 1990, the bassist, who went on to form the Rich Kids and play with Iggy Pop, published a book, I Was a Teenage Sex Pistol, about his experiences.

SOPHOMORE ROCK HISTORY

[10 POINTS PER CORRECT ANSWER]

17. (d) Led Zeppelin. The robbery took place at the Drake Hotel.

18. (b) Chicago. Rather than simply titling their fourth album Chicago IV, the group released a four-disc boxed-set concert record (Chicago at Carnegie Hall). Fifteen years later, Bruce Springsteen would beat Chicago's record with a five-album live set that went to number one.

19. (b) Paul McCartney.

20. (d) Bing Crosby. Crosby died between the show's September taping and its December broadcast; in the winter of '82, the Bowie/Crosby duet became a U.K. hit single. (In a bizarre coincidence, Bowie had appeared on Marc Bolan's British TV show that same September, joining his old friend/rival for a duet on "Standing Next to You." Bolan was killed in a car crash a few days later.)

21. (a) Bruce Springsteen. After playing an April 29 show in Memphis, Springsteen and a bandmate took a cab to Graceland, where the novice superstar jumped a fence and headed up the driveway in the hopes of getting to meet the real McCoy. A guard showed Bruce off the property. (Elvis had a number of unexpected callers that year: Jerry Lee Lewis drove up to the gates of Graceland in November, waving a pistol and demanding—unsuccessfully—to see the King.)

SINGERS AND RINGERS

[10 POINTS PER CORRECT ANSWER]

22. (d) Bryan Ferry

23. (a) Ian Hunter

24. (a) Joey Ramone

25. (b) Brad Delp

26. (b) Ian Gillan

ODD MEN OUT

[5 POINTS PER RINGER, 5 POINTS PER BAND]

27. (d) Steve Howe, Genesis. Although he probably would have fit in musically with Genesis, Howe played guitar in Yes and, in the '80s, Asia.

28. (c) David Johansen, Aerosmith. Both Steven Tyler and the New York Dolls (later solo) singer were frequently likened to Mick Jagger, and the two groups did tour together in the mid-'70s, but David Jo never twirled scarves in the Boston band.

29. (a) Ritchie Blackmore, Black Sabbath. Although there are personnel ties between Blackmore's two monster metal bands, Deep Purple and Rainbow, the guitarist himself left Sabbath to its own dark devices.

30. (e) Robert Wyatt, Pink Floyd. The Soft Machine/Matching Mole/solo drummer/singer was never in Pink Floyd, although the Softs and the Floyd were both from the same wing of British psychedelia and played shows together at London's UFO Club.

31. (a) Denny Doherty, Wings. Unlike the two other Dennys (guitarist Laine and drummer Seiwell), singer Denny Doherty of the Mamas and the Papas was never a member of Paul McCartney's '70s band, Wings.

FAINT PRAISE AND DUBIOUS CLAIMS

[10 POINTS PER CORRECT ANSWER]

32. (a) Clash. The phrase was used by Epic Records in late 1978 for the American Give 'Em Enough Rope ad campaign. For what it's worth, the February 1978 Trouser Press contained a Clash article in which writer Pete Silverton had observed, "People only get into heavy duty arguments about bands that really matter."

33. (b) Keith Richards.

34. (d) The Rutles—Dirk, Stig, Nasty, and Barry—were a scathing Beatles parody devised by Eric Idle (Monty Python) and Neil Innes (Bonzo Dog Band) for a 1978 TV mockumentary. ("The Rutles story is a legend. A living legend. A legend that will

live a lifetime, long after lots of other living legends have died.") The soundtrack album contained songs like "Hold My Hand," "Ouch!" and "Piggy in the Middle"; there's even a tribute album (Rutles Highway Revisited) of the group's songs performed by others.

35. (c) Randy Newman.

36. (a) Frank Marino. The Texas-born leader and his Montreal-based group, Mahogany Rush, made eight albums in the '70s.

[1 POINT PER NICKNAME]

37. (a) Bruce Springsteen, Boss
(b) Clarence Clemons, Big Man
(c) David Bowie, Thin White Duke
(d) Jerry Garcia, Captain Trips
(e) John Bonham, Bonzo
(f) Nick Lowe, Basher
(g) Dr. John, Night Tripper
(h) Janis Joplin, Pearl
(i) Dale Griffin, Buffin
(j) Ronnie Lane, Plonk

ALBUMS YOU PROBABLY OWN

[10 POINTS PER CORRECT CHOICE]

38. (e) Doors, L. A. Woman

39. (c) Cheap Trick, In Color

40. (f) Michael Jackson, Off the Wall

41. (b) Clash, The Clash

42. (j) Rolling Stones, Exile on Main Street

DATES

[2 POINTS PER CORRECT ANSWER]

43. (a) 1975
(b) 1970
(c) 1971
(d) 1977
(e) 1973

[2 POINTS PER CORRECT ANSWER]

44. (a) 1974
(b) 1979
(c) 1970
(d) 1972
(e) 1976

[10 POINTS]

45. "That was the day that my daddy died."

UNDER THE COVERS

[2 POINTS PER CORRECT ANSWER]

46. (a) Hot Chocolate. "Brother Louie," written by Errol Brown and Tony Wilson, was a 1973 U.K. hit for the British group. Stories covered it a few months later and had an American number one.

(b) Al Green. "Take Me to the River," co-written by the great singer, first appeared on the 1974 album Al Green Explores Your Mind. Talking Heads did it on 1978's More Songs About Buildings and Food.

(c) Jackson 5. "Never Can Say Goodbye" was a monster J5 hit in April 1971, reportedly selling a million copies in five days. Isaac Hayes's version of the Clifton Davis song charted that June; Gloria Gaynor did the disco remake in 1974.

(d) B. J. Thomas. "Hooked on a Feeling," written by Mark James, was a hit for the

Texan country singer in 1968 and went gold a second time in 1974 when it was redone by the Swedish group Blue Swede, who borrowed its loopy arrangement (Ooga-chaka! Ooga! Ooga!) from a 1971 Jonathan King cover.

(e) Creedence Clearwater Revival. "Proud Mary," written by John Fogerty (who reportedly had never been anywhere near the Mississippi River), was a '69 million-seller for the group. In 1971, Ike and Tina Turner snagged a Grammy (best R&B vocal performance) for their accelerating live-in-a-Florida-studio recording of the song.

ROCKING ALL OVER THE WORLD

[1 POINT PER CORRECT IDENTIFICATION]

47. (a) Ace: British
(b) Rick Springfield: Australian
(c) Styx: American
(d) Eric Burdon: British
(e) Steely Dan: American
(f) Neil Young: Canadian
(g) Klaatu: Canadian
(h) Average White Band: British
(i) Mungo Jerry: British
(j) Nick Gilder: Canadian

[1 POINT PER CORRECT MATCH]

48. (a) "Woman from Tokyo"
(b) "The Night Chicago Died"
(c) "Get Out of Denver"
(d) "Please Come to Boston"
(e) "Hotel California"

[3 POINTS PER CORRECT ANSWER]

49. (a) "Philadelphia Freedom"
(b) "China Grove"
(c) "Mississippi Queen"

(d) "Detroit Rock City"
(e) "Ohio"

[10 POINTS]

50. (e) Montreux, Switzerland. In December 1971, a fire swept through the Casino in which the Mothers of Invention were scheduled to perform, destroying their equipment. Deep Purple, in town to play and record, wrote a song about the disaster. "Smoke on the Water" was included on Deep Purple's 1972 album Machine Head; a year later it became a hit single.

PAST LIVES

[10 POINTS PER CORRECT ANSWER]

51. (b) Jeff Beck Group. Fresh out of the Yardbirds in early 1967, Beck started a group with Rod Stewart and ex-Birds/Creation guitarist Wood, who took up bass for the duration. The trio shared stages with three different drummers for more than two tumultuous years.

52. (e) Elephant's Memory. Lennon and Ono were introduced to this "people's band," a radical group which had once included Carly Simon in its lineup and had released an album in 1970, by pre-yuppie Yippie Jerry Rubin. Besides its support sessions, Elephant's Memory cut a 1972 album of its own for Apple.

53. (d) Gary Lewis and the Playboys. Snuff Garrett produced many of Lewis's biggest songs; Oklahoma native Russell handled the musical arrangements. The future star also co-wrote "Everybody Loves a Clown" and "She's Just My Style" for Lewis.

54. (a) Neil Young. The Mynah Birds also included Young's future Buffalo Springfield bandmate Bruce Palmer and pre-Steppenwolf organist Goldy McJohn. According to The Guinness Encyclopedia of Popular Music, "In 1965, [Rick James] formed the Mynah Birds in New York . . . Motown signed the band as a riposte to the British wave of R&B artists then dominating the charts . . . their career was aborted when James was arrested for draft evasion."

55. (c) Modern Lovers. Jonathan Richman formed the Modern Lovers with Harrison, Robinson, and bassist Ernie Brooks around 1971. They quickly became darlings of America's nonexistent rock underground, and John Cale produced the demos—songs like "Roadrunner" and "She Cracked"—which ultimately became the group's first LP. By that point, Harrison and Brooks were playing with Elliott Murphy; Robinson joined the Cars. In 1977, after finishing Harvard, Harrison joined Talking Heads.

COVERS

[10 POINTS PER CORRECT ANSWER]

56. (d) Mick Fleetwood and Stevie Nicks do the pas de deux, although the tiny figures of John McVie and Mick Fleetwood—in a visual quote from the cover of 1975's Fleetwood Mac LP—appear in a crystal ball.

57. (a) Battersea Power Station. In his Pink Floyd biography, Saucerful of Secrets, the late Nicholas Schaffner notes that the flying pig in the photograph "drifted out of control and . . . was carried by prevailing winds over Heathrow Airport before finally crashing some twenty miles southeast of [London]."

58. (d) Charlie Watts. Wearing a breasty T-shirt, Uncle Sam top hat, white socks and no shoes, the jumping drummer is lofting a guitar in each hand in this David Bailey photograph.

59. (b) Underpants. Girls' knickers, to be exact—the disposable kind made of some paper towel product that was meant to be the trend of the future.

60. (e) Paul Simonon. The cover design was borrowed from Elvis Presley's eponymous 1956 debut, but the 1979 photo—by Pennie Smith—captures the Clash bassist about to pulverize his instrument on a New York stage.

61. (b) cat

IS IT LIVE?

[10 POINTS PER CORRECT ANSWER]

62. (d) It's Too Late to Stop Now

63. (b) Grateful Dead

64. (d) Rock n Roll Animal

65. (c) Time Fades Away

66.(a) Babylon by Bus

MOONLIGHTING

[10 POINTS PER CORRECT ANSWER]

67. (d) The Pirates of Penzance. In the summer of 1980, Ronstadt tried her hand at acting in a Central Park production of this Gilbert and Sullivan show. Pirates moved to Broadway and was later made into a movie, which also starred Ronstadt.

68.(a) Mick Jagger. His solo single of "Memo from Turner" b/w "Natural Magic" (both from the soundtrack of Performance) appeared in 1970. Bill Wyman made the group's first solo LP (Monkey Grip) in 1974; Keith Richards came in third, with a 1978 single of "Run Rudolph Run."

69. (d) Guitar playing. Robert Fripp—ex–King Crimson art-rocker, Brian Eno collaborator, Bowie sideman, etc., etc.—and some of his students joined forces on an all-acoustic 1978 album, billed as Robert Fripp and the League of Crafty Guitarists.

70. (e) Al Green. Christiane Bird, in The Jazz and Blues Lover's Guide to the U.S.: "The Reverend Al Green has a ministry at the Full Gospel Tabernacle (787 Hale Road) in Whitehaven, and when he shows up there's nothing quite like hearing that huge soul voice shake down this evil world. The only trouble is, there's no telling when he'll appear."

71. (b) Phil Rizzuto. The Scooter does a guest turn ("OK, here we go, we got a real pressure cooker going here . . .") on Meat Loaf's "Paradise by the Dashboard Light," sharing the overheated track with Ellen Foley, Todd Rundgren, Edgar Winter, and a roster of players and singers. Holy cow.

72. (c) Ian Stewart. An original in the incipient Rolling Stones (before Bill Wyman and Charlie Watts came along), the pianist was pushed out of the group by manager Andrew Oldham in 1963 but stuck around as a crypto-member until his death in 1985.

MOONLIGHTING IN PAIRS

[5 POINTS PER CORRECT ANSWER]

73. (b) Liza Minnelli and (d) Donovan. The diva can be heard on Muscle of Love's "Teenage Lament" and "Man with the Golden Gun" (Ronnie Spector, the Pointer Sisters, and part of Labelle also sing on that 1973 LP); Donovan is the only credited guest on Billion Dollar Babies, although Marc Bolan, Keith Moon, and other British rock celebs reportedly took part.

74. (a) Iggy Pop and (f) Lou Reed. Bowie produced a bunch of Iggy's records, including Raw Power, Lust for Life, and The Idiot. He co-produced Transformer (Reed) with Mick Ronson. Among his other production charges: Mott the Hoople, Carmen, and Dana Gillespie.

75. (b) Ringo Starr and (d) Michael Jackson. Everyone else on the list is guilty as charged.

NAMES

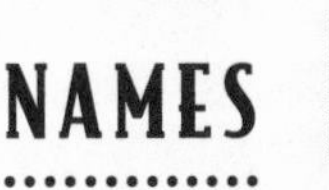

[10 POINTS PER CORRECT ANSWER]

76. (b) Power Station. The German group Kraftwerk (whose name translates as "Power Plant") first popularized techno-rock with the song "Autobahn."

77. (e) Bay City Rollers. The group name was allegedly chosen by sticking a pin into a map at random and landing on Bay City, Michigan.

78. (b) Artful Dodger. Although they never hit it big, the rocking pop group made four albums between 1975 and 1980. Uriah Heep was a British heavy metal band.

79. (d) "D'yer Mak'er."

[1 POINT PER CORRECT ANSWER]

80. (a) Alice Cooper
    (b) Elton John

(c) Elvis Costello
(d) Gene Simmons
(e) Meat Loaf
(f) Joe Strummer
(g) Chaka Khan
(h) Adam Ant
(i) Peter Wolf
(j) Marc Bolan

THE MANY FACES OF ROD STEWART

[2 POINTS PER CORRECT ANSWER]

81. (a) Faces did "Cindy Incidentally."
(b) Rod did "Maggie May."
(c) Rod did "Reason to Believe."
(d) Faces did "Stay with Me."
(e) Rod did "You Wear It Well."

82. (a) Rod (1970)
(b) Rod (1971)
(c) Faces (1971)
(d) Rod (1972)
(e) Faces (1973)

[1 POINT PER CORRECT ANSWER]

83. (a) Bob Dylan wrote "Only a Hobo" and recorded it for a 1963 compilation album, Broadside Ballads, Vol. 1.

(b) Eddie Cochran recorded "Cut Across Shorty," written by Marijohn Wilkin and Wayne Walker, in 1960.

(c) Chris Farlowe sang "My Way of Giving," a song written for him in 1967 by Steve Marriott and Ronnie Lane of the Small Faces, who also recorded it.

(d) Elton John co-wrote and recorded "Country Comfort" in 1970; Rod inexplicably pluralized the title when he put it on Gasoline Alley that year.

(e) The Temptations had a Top 10 hit with their 1966 rendition of Norman Whitfield/Eddie Holland/Cornelius Grant's "(I Know) I'm Losing You."

(f) Tim Hardin wrote "Reason to Believe" and sang it on his first album in 1966.

(g) Jimi Hendrix wrote and recorded "Angel," which was released posthumously on The Cry of Love (1971).

(h) Sam Cooke, a profound influence on Stewart's singing, wrote and recorded "Twistin' the Night Away," a 1962 million-seller.

(i) Maxine Brown recorded "Oh! No Not My Baby," a song written by Gerry Goffin and Carole King, in 1964; Manfred Mann did it in 1965.

(j) Etta James recorded "I'd Rather Go Blind," written by Ellington Jordan and Billy Foster, in 1967. Chicken Shack, with Christine Perfect (later McVie) as the featured vocalist, had a British hit with it in 1969.

NOVELTEASE

[10 POINTS PER CORRECT ANSWER]

84. (a) Loudon Wainwright III. "Dead Skunk" is the only hit he's ever had.

85. (d) "Desiderata." The well-deserved parody was "Deteriorata": "You are a fluke of the universe . . . you have no right to be here."

86. (e) Jaws. The gold-selling "Mr. Jaws" was only one in a long line of Goodman's inane cut-in classics: pre-sampling-era singles like "The Touchables," "Batman and His Grandmother," "Watergate," and "Superfly Meets Shaft" that answered corny setup lines with soundbites from other people's plastic. Goodman's career goes back to 1956, when he and Bill Buchanan came up with "The Flying Saucer" on the Luniverse label.

87. (a) "My Ding-a-Ling." By the time it was a hit, the song had been around the block more than a few times. Berry wrote it early in his career, recording it (as the even coyer "My Tambourine") in 1958. It was only when he redid it for The London Chuck Berry Sessions—recorded live in Coventry with a British band that included two future members of the Average White Band and an ex-Van der Graaf Generator bassist—that "My Ding-a-Ling" took off chartwise.

88.(d) Raspberries. Others records have used scratch-and-sniff covers, but the fruity aroma of Raspberries pervaded record shops in 1972, making it one of the few LPs in history that could be located in the dark by anyone with a nose.

BRUCE SPRINGSTEEN

[10 POINTS PER CORRECT ANSWER]

89.(c) Newsweek and Time.

90.(b) Patti Smith. Springsteen was working up "Because the Night" for Darkness at the Edge of Town in the same studio where the Patti Smith Group was recording Easter. She finished the lyrics and her band cut the song.

91. (e) The Wild, the Innocent & the E Street Shuffle. Not a single single was issued from Springsteen's second album, a collection of seven songs (including "Rosalita") that run between 4:26 and 9:56 in length.

92. (c) Manfred Mann's Earth Band. Although the Hollies had a small U.S. hit with "4th of July, Asbury Park (Sandy)" in 1975, Mann was the man who reached the top of the charts with "Blinded by the Light" at the end of 1976. The Pointer Sisters nearly did the trick with "Fire" in 1978; the Patti Smith Group's hit was also in '78.

93. (c) Southside Johnny and the Asbury Jukes. Springsteen was never in Johnny Lyons's band, but Southside did play harp in Dr. Zoom and the Sonic Boom before forming the Asbury Jukes.

ROCK AND ROLL AND ROCK AND ROLL

[1 POINT PER CORRECT ANSWER]

94.(a) "Rock and Roll Part 2" Gary Glitter
(b) "Rock and Roll All Nite" Kiss
(c) "Rock and Roll, Hoochie Koo" Rick Derringer

(d) "Rock'n'Roll Love Letter" Bay City Rollers
(e) "Rock & Roll Soul" Grand Funk Railroad
(f) "Rock 'n Roll with Me" David Bowie
(g) "Rock 'n' Roll Fantasy" Bad Company
(h) "A Rock 'N' Roll Fantasy" Kinks
(i) "Cities on Flame with Rock and Roll" Blue Öyster Cult
(j) "That's Rock 'n Roll" Eric Carmen

THE DISCO BEAT

[10 POINTS PER CORRECT ANSWER; 5 POINTS FOR EACH PART OF #100]

95. (b) Barry White. The Texan wrote "Harlem Shuffle" for Bob and Earl in the early '60s but made it big in the '70s with his own records, the vocal group Love Unlimited, and the Love Unlimited Orchestra. Hits under the White umbrella in 1973 included "Love's Theme," "I'm Gonna Love You Just a Little More Baby," and "Never, Never Gonna Give Ya Up."

96. (e) Football player. The "Macho Man" sextet did, however, include a biker, soldier, cowboy, construction worker, native American, and highway cop.

97. (a) Rick Dees. Along with His Cast of Idiots, Dees succeeded in making a parody record that was neither as good nor as funny as the genre it attempted to spoof.

98. (a) Beethoven's Fifth. The keyboardist's record was entitled "A Fifth of Beethoven." Poor Ludwig.

99. (c) Midnight Express. The synthmeister also did music for American Gigolo (1980), Foxes (1980), and Cat People (1982).

100a. (b) "Knock on Wood." After serving in the Broadway company of Bubbling Brown Sugar, Stewart was hired for the show's London production. She became a pop singer there; "Knock on Wood" was her second single.

100b. (c) Eddie Floyd co-wrote the song with guitarist Steve Cropper and cut it as a 1967 single. It was also the title track of his debut album.

CALIFORNIA SINGING

[5 POINTS]

101. Joni Mitchell. The song "California" is on her Blue album (1971).

[5 POINTS]

102. "The Air That I Breathe," co-written by Hammond and Mike Hazlewood for Phil Everly, became a Top 10 hit for the Hollies in 1974.

[3 POINTS PER NAME]

103a. The original incarnation of the Eagles was a quartet: Bernie Leadon (guitar/banjo/vocals), Glenn Frey (guitar/piano/vocals), Don Henley (drums/vocals), and Randy Meisner (bass/vocals).

[5 POINTS]

103b. Bernie Leadon was the first to leave the nest. He opted out after the fourth album (One of These Nights, 1975), by which time guitarist Don Felder had already been incorporated into the lineup.

[5 POINTS]

103c. Hotel California.

[5 POINTS FOR EACH PART]

104. Nicolette Larson, "Lotta Love" (a song from Young's Comes a Time LP)

[10 POINTS]

105. Bonnie Raitt. The Asher-produced The Glow was a success at the time, but nowhere near as big as Raitt's 1989 breakthrough, Nick of Time.

[8 POINTS]

106. Not a one.

FAMILY AFFAIRS

[5 POINTS]

107. Ramones. Despite the fictitious family name, no two Ramones—Joey (Hyman), Johnny (Cummings), Dee Dee (Colvin), Tommy (Erdelyi), Marky (Bell), Richie (Reinhardt), or C. J. (Ward)—are related.

[5 POINTS]

108. Fanny. The all-female rock quartet—purportedly America's first ever—made five albums; the two sisters subsequently cut a "solo" record. Ironically, when June Millington left the group, she was replaced by glam-rocker Suzi Quatro's elder sister, Patti.

[5 POINTS]

109. Paul McCartney. Mike McCartney adopted the McGear surname in the '60s in order to avoid identification, but it was never much of a secret. The two McCartneys co-wrote the songs for the McGear album (Mike's second solo LP), and Wings (Denny Laine, Jimmy McCullough, Linda McCartney) played on it.

[2 POINTS FOR EACH NAME]

110. Alex, Kate, and Livingston. Quite a dynasty.

[5 POINTS]

111. Edgar Winter toured and recorded with Johnny Winter's band in the early days. He's prominently featured on Second Winter.

[5 POINTS]

112. Jermaine. After the success of his first solo LP, Jermaine, the erstwhile J5 bassist took more than seven years to pay a return call on the Top 10: in 1980, "Let's Get Serious" did the trick.

[5 POINTS]

113a. 7.

[2 POINTS FOR EACH NAME]

113b. Alan, Jay, Merrill, Wayne, and Jimmy

BAD IDEAS AND ASSORTED BOONDOGGLES

[10 POINTS]

114. Kiss. Nowadays it would be medically unthinkable to play hemo-hype, but in 1977 it seemed like the heights (depths?) of wanton rock 'n' roll heaviosity to mix the band's blood into ink used to print Kiss's Marvel comic. Of course, it was all a publicity stunt, and no Kiss corpuscles were actually shed in the name of literature.

[10 POINTS]

115. Boomtown Rats. Mercury, soon to be the group's American ex-label, sent dead rats preserved in formaldehyde to radio stations. Needless to say, this stroke of marketing brilliance didn't help the band's career in the slightest.

[10 POINTS]

116. Klaatu. Named for the alien (not the robot Gort) in The Day the Earth Stood Still, this quartet of then-unidentified Canadian studio musicians who sounded an awful lot like the Beatles got a big career boost when a newspaper writer postulated their identities and set off a wave of speculation. It didn't hurt speculation that the cover of Ringo's 1974 LP, Goodnight Vienna, had Ringo dressed up as Klaatu.

[10 POINTS]

117a. David Bowie. At London's Hammersmith Odeon—the final stop on the Ziggy Stardust tour in July 1973, a gig documented with a film and a live LP—Bowie made his dramatic announcement before beginning the last number, "Rock 'N' Roll Suicide." "Not only is it the last show of the tour, but it's the last show that we'll ever do."

[5 POINTS]

117b. The Diamond Dogs tour began in June 1974. (Bowie's not the only one to pull the fake retirement gambit: Elton John did it in '77, starting up again in '79. And then there's the Who . . .)

[5 POINTS FOR EACH]

118. (b) Starland Vocal Band ("Afternoon Delight") and (j) Debby Boone, whose multimillion-selling, Grammy- and Oscar-winning hit was "You Light Up My Life."

RECIPES FOR CONSTRUCTION

[5 POINTS FOR EACH NAME]

119. Savoy Brown, Foghat. Singer/guitarist Dave Peverett, bassist Tone Stevens and drummer Roger Earl left Savoy Brown mainstay Kim Simmonds in the lurch after a financial disagreement, drafted singer/guitarist Rod Price, and became the gold-selling Foghat.

[3 POINTS FOR EACH NAME]

120. Free, Mott the Hoople, King Crimson. Paul Rodgers (vocals/guitar) and Simon Kirke (drums) were fresh out of Free, which had broken up in '73; guitarist Mick Ralphs got fed up with being in Mott the Hoople around the same time. Bassist Boz Burrell, ex-King Crimson (1970–1972), was "at liberty" before Bad Co.

[10 POINTS]

121. Emerson, Lake and Palmer. Keith Emerson (keyboards) came from the Nice, a group that laid the groundwork for ELP. Greg Lake had been the singer on King Crimson's first two albums (but bassist on only one). Drummer Carl Palmer came straight outta Atomic Rooster.

[10 POINTS]

122. Zombies. After the Zombies broke up (but before the posthumously released "Time of the Season," which keyboardist Rod Argent wrote, became their biggest single), Argent formed his namesake group with guitarist Russ Ballard and future Kinks Rob Henrit and Jim Rodford. "Hold Your Head Up" was a hit in 1972; the following year's "God Gave Rock and Roll to You" became an FM radio staple.

[5 POINTS]

123a. Curved Air. The British band had been and gone once when American drummer Copeland joined in a 1974 relaunch. He stuck around until Curved Air ended for good at the end of 1976.

[5 POINTS EACH FOR UP TO TWO NAMES]

123b. Zoot Money's Big Roll Band (1964–1967), Dantalion's Chariot (1967–1968), Soft Machine (1968), Animals (1968), Neil Sedaka (1973–1974), David Essex (1974), Kevin Coyne (1975–1976), Kevin Ayers (1976–1977), Strontium 90 (1977). Summers (a.k.a. Somers) was 35 when he joined the Police.

COMMERCIALS

[10 POINTS PER CORRECT ANSWER]

124. "Anticipation." Her 1972 hit provided the perfect accompaniment to the tantalizingly slow flow of Heinz ketchup.

125. Honda motor scooters. "Walk on the Wild Side," a seamy sketch of several Andy Warhol superstars, somehow became a Top 20 single in 1973; in the next decade it was deemed suitable to flog bikes. Is nothing sacrilegious?

126. "Up, Up and Away." Jim Webb wrote the song for an abortive movie about a balloon trip; at the recommendation of Johnny Rivers, the Fifth Dimension recorded it for their second hit in mid-'67. When TWA bought rights to use the song in commercials, however, the company had it rerecorded by another group.

127. "I'd Like to Teach the World to Sing." British songsmiths Roger Cook and Roger Greenaway wrote the original number, which was retitled and adapted for Coca-Cola's use by two American songwriters. Full-length covers of the jingle were released by America's Hillside Singers and Britain's New Seekers at the end of 1971; both became U.S. hits, while the latter had a U.K. number one as well.

POSTHUMOUS SUCCESS

[5 POINTS]

128. Jim Croce. "Bad, Bad Leroy Brown," released in March 1973, reached the top of the charts in July; the two-year-old "Time in a Bottle," released as a single in October 1973, equaled the feat.

[10 POINTS]

129. Dirty Deeds Done Dirt Cheap. Although AC/DC's first Australian album was released in 1974, none made it to America until '76. Dirty Deeds (with songs like "Big Balls" and "Problem Child"), their third Australian LP, had not been issued here when Scott choked on his vomit in February '80. A year later, by which time the group had released Back in Black with ex-Geordie shrieker Brian Johnson in Scott's place, Dirty Deeds appeared and went platinum.

[5 POINTS FOR EACH PART]

130. Lynyrd Skynyrd, Street Survivors. Not only was the cover artwork deemed ghoulish under the circumstances, the group's sixth album included a mail-order merchandise form headlined "Lynyrd Skynyrd—Survival Kit" and a detailed four-month itinerary of the tour that ended when the group's plane went down in Mississippi after the fourth show. The cover was altered to remove the flames.

THE WHO

[5 POINTS FOR EACH]

131. Quadrophenia and Who Are You stand as the Who's biggest chart hits. Tommy, Live at Leeds, Who's Next, and Face Dances follow. Incidentally, the Who's entire career includes only one American Top 10 single: "I Can See for Miles."

[5 POINTS EACH]

132. "Shakin' All Over" (Johnny Kidd and the Pirates), "Summertime Blues" (Eddie Cochran), and "Young Man Blues" (Mose Allison).

[10 POINTS]

133. John Entwistle drew the connect-the-dots cartoon cover.

[10 POINTS]

134. Jimmy—joining Tommy and Billy in the Townshend song character list.

[5 POINTS]

135a. Two Sides of the Moon, with guest appearances by half the rock world (Dick Dale, Joe Walsh, Flo and Eddie, Ringo Starr, Rick Nelson, Harry Nilsson, John Sebastian, et al.), included the drummer's uniquely sung renditions of the Who's "The Kids Are Alright," the Beach Boys' "Don't Worry Baby," and the Beatles' "In My Life."

[5 POINTS]

135b. John Entwistle's Ox. ("The Ox" is the stolid bassist's nickname.) Entwistle's touring group consisted of Memphis guitarist Robert Johnson, drummer Graham Deakin, and keyboardist Mike Deacon.

[5 POINTS]

135c. Leo Sayer. Sayer hooked up with Daltrey when he recorded an album at the singer's studio. Daltrey asked Sayer and his partner, Dave Courtney, to write the song for his 1973 solo debut, Daltrey, which was then released prior to Sayer's LP.

[5 POINTS]

135d. "Going Mobile." The other song on the album that dispenses with Daltrey is "M Wife," a John Entwistle composition that he sings.

CAN I BORROW A SONG?

[5 POINTS EACH]

136. (a) David Bowie gave "All the Young Dudes" to Mott the Hoople (they were

offered "Suffragette City" but passed) as an inducement to keep the band together. Bowie also produced the 1972 album of the same title.

(b) Joni Mitchell, who didn't actually attend the festival, wrote "Woodstock" and included it on Ladies of the Canyon. Crosby, Stills, Nash and Young covered it for a hit, one of the few songs written outside the group that they ever recorded. Matthews Southern Comfort translated it for Britain and got a hit as well.

(c) Bob Marley wrote "Stir It Up," but by the time he put it on 1973's Catch a Fire, singer/actor Johnny Nash—who recorded in Jamaica but was actually from Texas—had already staked his claim to it.

(d) Randy Newman wrote "Mama Told Me (Not to Come)."

(e) Steve Goodman, Chicago-born folksinger/songwriter, composed "The City of New Orleans" during an Illinois train trip; Arlo Guthrie sang it in 1972. Goodman died in the mid-'80s.

[10 POINTS]

137. "He's So Fine." The publishing company that owned the copyright on the Chiffons' 1963 classic successfully sued Harrison in 1971. Odd bit of irony: "My Sweet Lord" was produced by Phil Spector, an auteur of girl-group records, although he never worked with the Chiffons.

[10 POINTS]

138. Van Halen. The quartet's irreverent rip through the Kinks' "You Really Got Me" jump-started the group's career. As Ray Davies recently noted, "Now, when the Kinks do it, kids come up and congratulate us on playing that Van Halen song."

[5 POINTS]

139a. Blondie. Although the group didn't make an appreciable commercial dent in America until 1979's "Heart of Glass," a single of "Denis," taken from the group's second album, Plastic Letters, became a U.K. hit in early 1978.

[5 POINTS]

139b. "Denise."

[10 POINTS]

140a. Nazareth. Other songs in their repertoire: Joni Mitchell's "This Flight Tonight," Bob Dylan's "The Ballad of Hollis Brown," Woody Guthrie's "Vigilante Man," and Tomorrow's "My White Bicycle."

[5 POINTS]

140b. "Love Hurts," written by Boudleaux Bryant, was first recorded by the Everly Brothers in 1960 on A Date with the Everly Brothers.

MORE SONG BUSINESS

[5 POINTS]

141. Brownsville Station. Guitarist Cub Koda led this boisterous group from Ann Arbor, Michigan, throughout the '70s. Despite seven LPs and an endless amount of roadwork, B.S. had only two hits: "Smokin' in the Boys Room" (1973) and "Kings of the Party" (1974).

[5 POINTS]

142. "Bridge Over Troubled Water." Simon and Garfunkel's original rendition of the song reached number one and won a Record of the Year Grammy in 1970.

[5 POINTS]

143. James Taylor.

[5 POINTS]

144. "Good Times" by Chic. That chart-topping single from the summer of '79 provided the instrumental foundation of "Rapper's Delight" and bears more than a passing resemblance to the rhythm and bass part of Queen's "Another One Bites the Dust" (1980).

[5 POINTS]

145. "Lucy in the Sky with Diamonds." Elton John and John Lennon (playing guitar

under the pseudonym Dr. Winston O'Boogie) collaborated on this in 1974. Lennon joined John onstage at Madison Square Garden that November; their live version of "I Saw Her Standing There" was released as a B-side.

PEOPLE WHO SING ABOUT PEOPLE

[5 POINTS]

146a. "Sweet Home Alabama," by Lynyrd Skynyrd, contains the lyric "I hope Neil Young will remember / A southern man don't need him around anyhow."

[5 POINTS]

146b. "Southern Man." "Southern man, better keep your head, don't forget what your Good Book says."

[5 POINTS]

146c. "Walk On," from On the Beach. "I hear some people been talking me down . . ." Still, Young, quoted in Cameron Crowe's liner notes for One More from the Road, acknowledged that "I'm proud to have my name in a song like theirs." (A song like theirs?)

[5 POINTS]

147. Syd Barrett. Roger Waters wrote and sang the lyrics to reflect "that sort of indefinable, inevitable melancholy about the disappearance of Syd." Syd himself turned up unexpectedly at the studio during the mixing sessions for the song.

[10 POINTS]

148a. Bruce Johnston. The sometime Beach Boy bassist and producer wrote the song. David Cassidy had a British hit with it before Barry Manilow topped the American charts with it in early '76.

[5 POINTS]

148b. Brian Wilson.

[5 POINTS]

149. Duke Ellington. The song "Sir Duke" also tips a hat to Count Basie and Ella Fitzgerald, among others.

[2 POINTS FOR EACH CORRECT MATCH]

150. (a) Bob Dylan: "George Jackson." Dylan wrote a song about this imprisoned African-American radical shortly after Jackson was killed in 1971.

(b) John Lennon: "John Sinclair." The White Panther party founder/MC5 mentor was incarcerated for a pot charge in 1969.

(c) Brian Wilson: "Johnny Carson."

(d) Ian Dury: "Sweet Gene Vincent." The leather-clad rocker is best remembered for 1956's "Be-Bop-a-Lula."

(e) David Bowie: "Andy Warhol." Bowie also did "Song for Bob Dylan."

(f) Jonathan Richman: "Pablo Picasso," who, the lyrics declare, "was never called an asshole."

(g) Alice Cooper: "Ballad of Dwight Fry." Frye (Coop, who co-wrote the song with guitarist Michael Bruce, misspelled the name) was the American film actor who played Renfrew in the classic 1931 Dracula.

(h) Todd Rundgren: "Wolfman Jack." Other than this and the Del-Lords' "Saint Jake" (about Jack Spector), how many odes to disc jockeys can there be?

(i) Nick Lowe: "Marie Provost." Lowe misspelled the name of this silent-screen star whose sad end was described in Hollywood Babylon. Quoth St. Nick: "She was a winner that became a doggie's dinner."

(j) Van Morrison: "Jackie Wilson Said (I'm in Heaven When You Smile)." Don't be misled: the parenthetical lyric is Morrison's, not Wilson's. What Jackie Wilson said was "Reet Petite."

GLAM ROCK AND GLITTER

[2 POINTS PER BAND IDENTIFICATION; 1 POINT PER SONG TITLE]

151. (a) Roxy Music: "Virginia Plain," 1972
 (b) Sparks: "This Town Ain't Big Enough for Both of Us," 1974
 (c) T. Rex: "Bang a Gong (Get It On)," 1971
 (d) Mott the Hoople: "All the Young Dudes," 1972
 (e) David Bowie: "Rebel Rebel," 1974
 (f) David Essex: "Rock On," 1973
 (g) Slade: "Mama Weer All Crazee Now," 1972
 (h) Sweet: "Blockbuster," 1973
 (i) Wizzard: "See My Baby Jive," 1973
 (j) Gary Glitter: "I Didn't Know I Loved You (Till I Saw You Rock and Roll)," 1972

NAMESAKES

[2 POINTS PER CORRECT ANSWER]

152. (a) J. Geils: guitar
 (b) Larry Graham: bass
 (c) Harry "K.C." Casey: keyboards
 (d) Brinsley Schwarz: guitar
 (e) Robert "Kool" Bell: bass
 (f) Ronnie Montrose: guitar

[1 POINT PER CORRECT ANSWER]

153. (b) Larry Graham
 (c) Harry Casey
 (e) Robert "Kool" Bell. (When James Taylor [not that James Taylor] joined the group in 1978, he took over lead vocals.)

HEAVY METAL

[1 POINT PER BAND CORRECTLY IDENTIFIED]

154. (a) Judas Priest
(b) Motörhead
(c) Deep Purple
(d) Scorpions
(e) AC/DC
(f) UFO
(g) Uriah Heep
(h) Triumph
(i) Blue Öyster Cult
(j) Nazareth

[1 POINT PER BAND CORRECTLY IDENTIFIED]

155. (a) Rush: Caress of Steel (1975)
(b) Blue Öyster Cult: Some Enchanted Evening (1978)
(c) Judas Priest: Sad Wings of Destiny (1976)
(d) Black Sabbath: Technical Ecstasy (1976)
(e) Scorpions: Fly to the Rainbow (1974)
(f) Ritchie Blackmore's Rainbow: Long Live Rock'n'Roll (1978)
(g) Triumph: Rock'n'Roll Machine (1979)
(h) Mountain: Twin Peaks (1974)
(i) Golden Earring: Mad Love (1977)
(j) Angel: Helluva Band (1976)

[10 POINTS]

156. April Lawton.

THANKS, I'LL REMAKE IT MYSELF

[10 POINTS]

157. Bryan Ferry. The Roxy Music crooner's third solo LP included his re-renditions of "Casanova," "Sea Breezes," "2 H.B.," "Chance Meeting," and "Re-make/Re-model." He wrote all the songs, which, except for "Casanova" (from Country Life), are from Roxy's first LP.

[10 POINTS]

158. Electric Light Orchestra. Jeff Lynne's "Do Ya" was originally waxed by the Move in its waning days (1972). Lynne then followed Move maestro Roy Wood into ELO, where he recut the song after Wood left. Incidentally, Todd Rundgren's Utopia recorded "Do Ya" live in '75 as a payback for the Move once playing "Open My Eyes."

[5 POINTS PER SONG TITLE]

159. "Black Mountain Side" and "Over the Hills and Far Away." Both songs recycle guitar parts from "White Summer," a Jimmy Page showcase on the Yardbirds' Little Games LP. (The previously unreleased acoustic version included on the Little Games Sessions & More reissue makes this perfectly clear.)

[10 POINTS]

160. "Castles in the Air." McLean first recorded it for his 1970 debut album, Tapestry; issued several times as a single, the song struck paydirt in '72. Nine years later, McLean tried a more intricate arrangement of the song for the Believers album.

[10 POINTS]

161. "Ready for Love." Ralphs originally wrote and sang the song (as a medley with "After Lights") on Mott the Hoople's All the Young Dudes. Paul Rodgers sang it on Bad Company.

[5 POINTS FOR THE BAND, 5 POINTS FOR THE TITLE]

162. Cheap Trick, "I Want You to Want Me." The song initially appeared on Trick's second LP, In Color, but it was the live version from Cheap Trick at Budokan (recorded

in Tokyo in April 1978) that made lots of people want to want the song.

SURFING A NEW WAVE

[10 POINTS]

163. "Video Killed the Radio-Star." Written by Trevor Horn and Geoffrey Downes (a.k.a. the Buggles) and Bruce Woolley, the song was recorded by both Woolley (and the Camera Club) and the Buggles (on their first LP, The Age of Plastic). It was the latter's version whose video inaugurated the era of music television.

[10 POINTS]

164. "Carbona Not Glue." Not to be confused with "Now I Wanna Sniff Some Glue," a song from the brudders' first album, this one ran into trademark problems with the chemical company and was wiped off the LP.

[5 POINTS PER BAND]

165. Television and the Heartbreakers. A band that bassist/singer Hell (né Lester Meyers) formed with guitarist Tom Verlaine in 1971 transmuted into Television in 1973. Hell split in '75; Marquee Moon, Television's first LP, appeared in '77. Hell then formed the Heartbreakers with Johnny Thunders and Jerry Nolan (both ex–New York Dolls) but left before the Heartbreakers moved to England and got a record deal.

[5 POINTS]

166a. Linda Ronstadt. The album she built around them was Mad Love.

[1 POINT PER TITLE]

166b. "Party Girl," "Girls Talk," and "Talking in the Dark" are on Mad Love; "Alison" was on Living in the USA.

[10 POINTS]

167. The Damned. Damned Damned Damned was released in February 1977; the group's first U.S. tour was in April '77. Hardly the best, but surely the first.

[10 POINTS]

168. Give 'Em Enough Rope. This was actually the Clash's second album. The group's American label passed on releasing its debut and got on the ball only with its 1978 follow-up. Wisely, Epic changed its tune in 1979 and, after making significant alterations to the contents, gave The Clash its belated release.

[10 POINTS]

169. The Selecter. As George Marshall tells it in The Two Tone Story, the Specials "only had enough money to record one track . . . Neol Davies was offered the chance to be on the single." So "The Selecter," an instrumental the guitarist had written and recorded with future Specials drummer John Bradbury, was touched up and stuck on the B-side, credited to the Selecter. When the 45 took off, Davies put an actual group together.

[5 POINTS]

170a. Stiff. Check out Stiff: The Story of a Record Label by Bert Muirhead and The Stiff Records Box Set for complete details on the world's most flexible (defunct) record label.

[5 POINTS]

170b. Akron, Ohio. The album was an are-there-any-more-at-home-like-you? response to Devo, Stiff's own Akron spudboys. The Akron Compilation contained tracks by Tin Huey, Rubber City Rebels, Jane Aire and the Belvederes, and other local legends.

[2 POINTS]

170c. Tires. As lovely as it sounds.

[1 POINT FOR EACH CORRECT ANSWER]

171. (a) Johnnie Fingers played keyboards in the Boomtown Rats.
(b) Steve Nieve was the keyboard wiz for Elvis Costello and the Attractions.
(c) Rat Scabies drummed in the Damned.
(d) Billy Zoom was the guitarist in X.

(e) Darby Crash was the singer in the Germs.
(f) Poly Styrene was the singer in X-Ray Spex.
(g) Jet Black drums for the Stranglers.
(h) Lux Interior is the singer of the Cramps.
(i) Cheetah Chrome played guitar in the Dead Boys.
(j) Top Ten was the rhythm guitarist in the Dictators.

YOU MUST RE-MEMBER THIS

[1 POINT PER MEMBER NAMED]

172. Mick Fleetwood (drums, 1967–), Bob Brunning (bass, 1967), Peter Green (guitar/vocals, 1967–1970, 1971), Jeremy Spencer (guitar/vocals, 1967–1971), John McVie (bass, 1967–), Danny Kirwan (guitar/vocals, 1968–1972), Christine Perfect McVie (keyboards/vocals, 1970–), Bob Welch (guitar/vocals, 1971–1974), Bob Weston (guitar/vocals, 1972–1973), Dave Walker (vocals, 1972–1973), Stevie Nicks (vocals, 1975–), Lindsey Buckingham (guitar/vocals, 1975–1987), Billy Burnette (guitar/vocals, 1987–), Rick Vito (guitar/vocals, 1987–1991).

[5 POINTS FOR EACH CORRECT CHOICE]

173. (b) Crosby/Nash and (e) Stills/Young.

[2 POINTS PER DRUMMER]

174. (a) Bev Bevan. Bevan was a founding member of both the Move and the Electric Light Orchestra. He toured (but did not record) with Black Sabbath in the mid-'80s.

(b) Carmine Appice. He began his career with Vanilla Fudge, then formed Cactus (with Fudge bassist Tim Bogert) in 1969. In the late '70s, he joined Rod Stewart's band.

(c) Aynsley Dunbar. The British drummer, who had been in John Mayall's

Bluesbreakers, was a 1967 member of the Jeff Beck Group. He later moved to America, joined the Mothers of Invention, Journey, and then the Jefferson Starship.

(d) Bill Bruford. He was the first drummer in Yes, the fourth drummer in King Crimson, and a 1976 touring member of Genesis.

(e) Marc Bell. He started off in early-'70s heavy rockers Dust, then joined the New York underground in Richard Hell's Voidoids. In 1978, he changed his name to Marky Ramone and joined the Ramones.

[5 POINTS EACH]

175. Bunny Livingston (later known as Bunny Wailer) and Peter Tosh (real name: Winston MacIntosh). Formed in the mid-'60s, the Wailers disbanded and was re-formed by the central trio in 1967.

[1 POINT PER NAME]

176. Blondie Chaplin, Ricky Fataar, Alan Jardine, Mike Love, Brian Wilson, Carl Wilson, and Dennis Wilson. Each is credited with composing at least one of the album's songs.

PRODUCERS

[1 POINT PER PRODUCER CORRECTLY IDENTIFIED]

177. (a) George "Shadow" Morton. Morton's career began in 1964 with the Shangri-Las. He oversaw all the Vanilla Fudge's late-'60s albums and took the controls for the Dolls' second LP, In Too Much Too Soon (1974).

(b) Chris Thomas. He produced early albums by Climax Chicago Blues Band in the late '60s; the Sex Pistols (co-credited to Bill Price) was only one of dozens of prestige projects (Badfinger, Procol Harum, Roxy Music, Pretenders) he took on in the '70s.

(c) Tony Visconti. The Brooklynite began working with Marc Bolan when Tyrannosaurus Rex was still an acoustic duo; he stuck around long enough to produce most of the electric warrior's hits. While no one is listed as producer of Iggy Pop's 1977 LP, The Idiot, Visconti mixed it; David Bowie took a "recorded by" credit.

(d) George Martin. The Beatles were a big job, but Martin found time to produce other bands in the '60s, including a couple of albums for another Mersey band, Billy

J. Kramer and the Dakotas. Martin produced Blow by Blow and Wired for Beck; other modern bands to get Martinized include Cheap Trick and Ultravox.

(e) Guy Stevens. Better known as the Mott the Hoople mastermind, Stevens produced Free's first album, Tons of Sobs, in 1967. A decade later, he returned from obscurity to clash with the Clash over London's Calling.

[3 POINTS FOR EACH CORRECT ANSWER]

178. (a) Fabulous Poodles. Entwistle produced their eponymous 1977 debut, some tracks of which appeared on the American Mirror Stars compilation.

(b) Tucky Buzzard. Wyman produced a bunch of early-'70s LPs by this English band (at least one of which, Allright on the Night, is worth hearing).

(c) Lon and Derrek Van Eaton. Beatles associate Voorman produced Brother, released on Apple, for this fraternal group in 1973.

(d) Roy Buchanan. Stanley Clarke produced 1977's Loading Zone for the late guitarist.

(e) Jorma Kaukonen. Hot Tuna bandmate Casady took the helm for the ex-Airplane guitarist's first solo album (with Tom Hobson), Quah, in 1974.

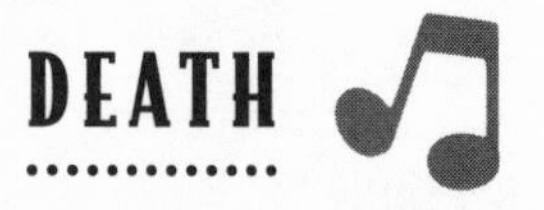

[1 POINT FOR EACH CORRECT YEAR]

179. (a) Sid Vicious (1979)
(b) Gram Parsons (1973)
(c) Phil Ochs (1976)
(d) Berry Oakley (1972)
(e) Keith Moon (1978)
(f) Mama Cass Elliott (1974)
(g) Tim Buckley (1975)
(h) Marc Bolan (1977)

INSTRUMENTALS

[5 POINTS EACH]

180. "Dueling Banjos" and "Frankenstein." Eric Weissberg and Steve Mandell did the five-string tussle for the soundtrack of Deliverance, while the Edgar Winter Group rocked out in the name of the monster.

[5 POINTS]

181. George Benson. The highly rated jazz guitarist, who had sung early in his long career, won an instrumental Grammy for his 1976 LP, Breezin'. That same year, he was ranked top jazz guitarist in three major readers' polls. In 1978, he won a Grammy in the R&B Vocal category for "On Broadway."

[5 POINTS EACH]

182. Tubular Bells, The Exorcist. With some instrumental assistance, 19-year-old Mike Oldfield pieced together Tubular Bells on an assortment of guitars and keyboards. The British chart-topping album was released Stateside, but it didn't take off until an excerpt used in The Exorcist was issued as a single in '74.

THE MOVIES

[10 POINTS]

183. Stray Cats. Brian Setzer's rockabilly revival was not yet under way (the guitarist was barely a teenager in 1974) when the cinematic Stray Cats had their fictional moment of glory. Once the actual New York band emigrated to London in 1980, however, Edmunds became their producer.

[10 POINTS]

184. The Carrie Nations. The bodacious trio was played by Dolly Read, Cynthia Myers, and Marcia McBroom. The film also has an on-screen appearance by the Strawberry Alarm Clock.

[10 POINTS]

185. Nik Cohn. The original article ("Another Saturday Night") about Brooklyn disco dancers was in New York magazine. The venerable rock critic also influenced Pete Townshend to write a song about a pinball wizard; in 1970 Cohn published a novel entitled Arfur, Teenage Pinball Queen.

[2 POINTS FOR EACH ONE—UP TO FIVE—NAMED]

186. The complete list: Superfly ('72), Claudine ('74), Let's Do It Again ('75), Sparkle ('76), A Piece of the Action ('77), and Short Eyes ('77).

SINGLES CLUB

[5 POINTS]

187. Boomtown Rats. The fact-based "I Don't Like Mondays," whose title was the explanation given by an American schoolgirl for an unprovoked shooting spree, is the closest thing to a U.S. hit the Rats could show for six good-to-great albums.

[5 POINTS]

188a. What's Going On.

[2 POINTS PER SONG TITLE]

188b. "What's Going On," "Mercy Mercy Me (The Ecology)," and "Inner City Blues (Make Me Wanna Holler)."

[10 POINTS]

189. "Money." Released in 1973, it spent two measly months in the Top 40 charts and didn't even reach the Top 10. A follow-up, "Us and Them," didn't break the Top 100! Go figure. (In Britain, no single was released from Dark Side.)

[10 POINTS]

190. Todd Rundgren, "Hello It's Me," a remake of a song Rundgren originally recorded with his band Nazz.

[2 POINTS PER SONG TITLE]

191. "Go Your Own Way," "Dreams," "Don't Stop," "You Make Loving Fun." Lindsey Buckingham wrote the first one, Stevie Nicks the second; the other two are by Christine McVie.

[10 POINTS]

192. "You Ain't Seen Nothing Yet." Randy Bachman's vocal was recorded as a joke for Bachman-Turner Overdrive's stammering manager and not meant to be a final version. Somehow, the track was released as stuttered. It's not clear who had the last laugh.

[5 POINTS EACH FOR THE EAGLE AND THE TITLE]

193. Glenn Frey, "New Kid in Town." The first two singles were "Hotel California" and "Life in the Fast Lane."

[10 POINTS]

194. "Good Girls Don't." The Knack went a bit too far with this one. In the 45 version, the song's unnamed babe "puts you in your place" rather than "sitting on your face" and is "giving you a chance" rather than letting you "get inside her pants." Radio listeners didn't know, but little album buyers understood.

SONG CHARACTERS, REAL AND IMAGINED

[2 POINTS FOR EACH NAME]

195. Wayne Kramer, Peter Green, and Keith Richards. MC5 guitarist Kramer spent two years in the joint for a cocaine conviction. Ex–Fleetwood Mac guitarist Green was institutionalized in 1977 after assaulting an accountant who was bringing him a royalty check. Keith Richards has attracted the interest of many constabularies over the years.

[10 POINTS]

196. "an underworld spy or the wife of a close friend."

[10 POINTS]

197. Botticelli, the fifteenth-century Italian painter.

[10 POINTS]

198. "Keith Don't Go (Ode to the Glimmer Twin)," a song for Keith Richards.

[1 POINT FOR EACH SONG TITLE, 1 POINT FOR EACH ARTIST]

199. (a) "Telegram Sam," Marc Bolan/T. Rex
(b) "50 Ways to Leave Your Lover," Paul Simon
(c) "Drive-In Saturday," David Bowie
(d) "Incident on 57th Street," Bruce Springsteen
(e) "Surrender," Cheap Trick. (If you don't hear it right away, the entire band gets a namecheck near the end of the song. Robin sings "Bun E.'s alright, Tom's alright," etc. before dissolving into a steady round of "we're all alright.")

[2 POINTS PER LEGEND—UP TO 5]

200. The complete list: Greta Garbo, Rudolph Valentino, Bela Lugosi, Bette Davis, George Sanders, Mickey Rooney, and Marilyn (Monroe).

HAVE A NICE DECADE

[5 POINTS PER QUESTION; 10 POINTS FOR #206]

201. "The Streak" by Ray Stevens. This ditty about the quaint fad of naked jogging sprinted up the charts shortly after a streaker brought the phenomenon home to America's living rooms via an unscheduled Academy Awards appearance.

202. Police siren. Apparently enough people hearing the song on their car radios were convinced they were being pulled over that the record company decided to edit out the siren for the benefit of broadcasters.

203. Michael Murphey. The so-called cosmic cowboy's equine ode was "Wildfire."

204. Lead singer Tony Burrows. Edison Lighthouse, White Plains, and Pipkins were all ephemeral studio concoctions for whom voice-for-hire Burrows—a onetime member of the Ivy League and the Flowerpot Men—sang what became their big hits in 1970. The Brotherhood of Man was a more substantial outfit that released records throughout the '70s.

205. Jerry Leiber and Mike Stoller. The authors of such classic '50s songs as "Hound Dog," "Kansas City," and "Riot in Cell Block #9" produced the Drifters, the Coasters, Jay and the Americans, and many others before happening upon Stealers Wheel in the early '70s.

206. "Listen to What the Man Said," a single from the Venus and Mars LP. Interestingly, Paul McCartney's similar 17-song All the Best! collection includes that song but omits "Hi, Hi, Hi" and "Mull of Kintyre."

FLIPSIDES

[5 POINTS PER CORRECT ANSWER; 5 POINTS FOR EACH PART OF #209 AND #210]

207. "Season in the Sun" by Terry Jacks. Ostensibly about a woman asking her butcher for a favor on behalf of her injured dog, the simple lyrics include "The meat from the pork is sweet... Put the bone in, she begged him, as she paced around the

floor." Soul Asylum included their boisterous rendition of the song as a "special bone-us track" on their 1988 album, Hang Time.

208. "American Pie." While the full version of Don McLean's saga of "the day the music died" took up both sides of a 7-inch, a truncated version was released at the same time (October 1971) with "Empty Chairs" on the flip.

209a. "Cruel to Be Kind."

209b. Brinsley Schwarz. Lowe (bass/vocals) and Gomm (guitar/vocals) played together (1970–1975) in the countryish pub-rock band led by future Rumour guitarist Schwarz. The first "Cruel to Be Kind" backed up Lowe's 1978 single, "Little Hitler."

210. "Silver Train," "Angie."

SEX PISTOLS

[2 POINTS PER LABEL]

211. EMI, A&M, Virgin. The song "EMI" also mentions A&M, the label that didn't release any Pistols product. (Although A&M did press copies of "God Save the Queen" in 1977, the band wasn't on the label long enough for any to reach the shops.)

[5 POINTS]

212a. Bill Grundy. As the host of Thames Television's Today show, Grundy interviewed the Pistols as a last-minute replacement for Queen.

[5 POINTS]

212b. Siouxsie Sioux (Susan Dallion) was a member of the Bromley Contingent, a group of early Pistols fans that also numbered Billy Idol. She was among those in the studio during the broadcast and participated in the row with Grundy.

[5 POINTS PER CITY]

213. Atlanta and San Francisco. In the course of 10 days, the Pistols came, were seen, and collapsed, with half the band on its way to Brazil and Sid Vicious in a New York hospital, comatose from a drug overdose.

[5 POINTS PER SONG]

214. "Something Else" and "C'mon Everybody." Both were 1979 British singles, with Sid Vicious on lead vocals. (While Eddie Cochran had a "My Way," the Pistols did the Paul Anka/Frank Sinatra tune instead.) Other covers in the Pistols' holster: "Substitute" (Who), "Roadrunner" (Modern Lovers), "(I'm Not Your) Steppin' Stone" (Monkees), "Rock Around the Clock" (Bill Haley), "Whatcha' Gonna Do About It?" (Small Faces), and "No Fun" (Stooges).

STAGE DIVERSE

[10 POINTS PER CORRECT ANSWER; 2 POINTS PER CORRECT SONG IN #218; 1 POINT PER CORRECT BAND IN #219]

215. Having Fun with Elvis on Stage. From Elvis: The Illustrated Record by Roy Carr and Mick Farren: "Bottom-of-the-barrel scrapings of the worst kind. . .if God had wanted Elvis to be a professional comedian, he would have given him a funny nose, baggy pants, a banana skin and an exploding guitar."

216. Eric Clapton. Eric Clapton's Rainbow Concert, a record of the all-star gig at London's Rainbow Theatre, features such songs as "Badge," "Presence of the Lord," "After Midnight," and "Little Wing."

217. John Siomos (drums), Bob Mayo (guitar/keyboards), Stanley Sheldon (bass). Any of them will do.

218. "A Hard Rain's A-Gonna Fall," "It Takes a Lot to Laugh, It Takes a Train to Cry," "Blowin' in the Wind," "Mr. Tambourine Man," and "Just Like a Woman." The concert was held at Madison Square Garden on August 1, 1971; George Harrison's casual introduction was "I'd like to bring on a friend of us all, Mr. Bob Dylan."

219. Sex Pistols, Clash, Damned, Buzzcocks, Siouxsie and the Banshees, Subway Sect, Chris Spedding, Vibrators, and, from France, Stinky Toys.

NAME THAT TUNESMITH

[4 POINTS PER CORRECT ANSWER]

220. (a) Pete Townshend. "Love Is Coming Down" is on Who Are You; "Mother and Son" was written and recorded for the film soundtrack of Tommy; "Misunderstood" is a Townshend song on Rough Mix, his joint LP with Ronnie Lane; and "Too Much of Anything" is a 1972 Who outtake collected on Odds and Sods.

(b) Bruce Springsteen. Springsteen never released any of these commercially. "Talk to Me," a Darkness on the Edge of Town outtake, was covered by Southside Johnny and the Jukes; "Janey Needs a Shooter" was rewritten and recorded by Warren Zevon as "Jeannie Needs a Shooter"; "If I Was the Priest" was recorded by Allan Clarke of the Hollies; "Rendezvous," a Springsteen concert item of the mid-'70s, was recorded by Greg Kihn.

(c) David Bowie. "A New Career in a New Town" is on Low; "Candidate" is on Diamond Dogs; "Right" is on Young Americans; "Word on a Wing" is on Station to Station.

(d) Bob Dylan. "Something There Is About You" is on Planet Waves; "Golden Loom" was recorded by Roger McGuinn on his Thunderbyrd LP; "Sign Language" was done by Eric Clapton (with Dylan guesting) on No Reason to Cry; "Buckets of Rain," from Blood on the Tracks, was covered by Bette Midler with help from Dylan.

(e) Paul McCartney. "Girlfriend" is on London Town; "Wonderful Christmastime" was a 1979 seasonal single; "Warm and Beautiful" is on Wings at the Speed of Sound; "What Do We Really Know?" was written and recorded for his brother Mike's McGear LP.

[10 POINTS]

221. Billy Swan. "I Can Help," the song that brought the Missouri roustabout his moment of fame in 1974, was written and recorded after Kris Kristofferson presented him with a keyboard for a wedding gift. Presley included the song on 1975's Elvis Today.

[5 POINTS PER CORRECT ANSWER IN THIS THREE-PARTER]

222. (a) Billy Joel. The song, "Piano Man," became his first hit single in 1974.

(b) Bill Martin. Martin is his middle name.

(c) "Say Goodbye to Hollywood." Ronnie Spector recorded the track—a Ronettes homage Joel wrote when he moved back east in the mid-'70s—with the E Street Band in 1977.

[2 POINTS PER CORRECT ANSWER]

223. (a) Harry Nilsson. Nilsson Sings Newman appeared in 1970.

(b) Joni Mitchell put words to four new Mingus compositions and wrote some tributes of her own on Mingus, an LP released in 1979, the year of the jazz great's death.

(c) Denny Laine (or Raw). Obscure British band Raw devoted a 1971 LP (Raw Holly) to the Lubbock legend's songs; Holly Days, Laine's 1973 collaboration with Wings bandmates Paul and Linda McCartney, took a bit longer to reach the bargain bins.

(d) Hollies. OK, so Hollies Sing Dylan was actually released in May 1969. Rather than split hairs, the Byrds (The Byrds Play Dylan was issued at the start of 1980) is an acceptable answer.

(e) Willie Nelson. Nelson recorded To Lefty from Willie as a tribute to the influential early country star, who died in 1975.

[5 POINTS PER CORRECT ANSWER IN THIS THREE-PARTER]

224. (a) Gary Osborne. When Elton's partnership with Bernie Taupin went kablooey in 1976, Osborne, a lyricist who had written for Kiki Dee, stepped in. Their songwriting collaboration produced the 1978 LP A Single Man.

(b) "Grow Some Funk of Your Own" and "I Guess That's Why They Call It the Blues."

(c) Victim of Love. One of the biggest stiffs of Elton's career, this 1979 LP consisted of six songs written by producer Pete Bellotte with various others and an 8-minute version of "Johnny B. Goode."

FAR GONE AND OUT

[2 POINTS PER CORRECT ANSWER]

225. (a) Blondie. Bassist Valentine, who wrote "(I'm Always Touched by Your) Presence, Dear" for the group's second album, left after its first.

(b) Clash. When the drummer quit before The Clash's release, he was omitted from the cover photo and billed in the credits as "Tory Crimes." Five years later, he was chosen to replace his replacement, Topper Headon.

(c) Squeeze. Kakoulli was the original bassist; after two LPs, John Bentley took over.

(d) Duran Duran. Duffy, who made U.K. hits as Tin Tin before forming the Lilac Time, was the group's original vocalist. Simon Le Bon was its third.

(e) Jethro Tull. The guitarist played on Tull's jazzy/bluesy debut but left to form the jazzier Blodwyn Pig in 1969.

[4 POINTS PER CORRECT ANSWER]

226. (a) Back Street Crawler. After making a solo album entitled Back Street Crawler, the guitarist used the name for the mid-'70s group he led until his death. (There's an alternate correct answer: Free split temporarily in 1971, during which time Kossoff formed a quartet with Simon Kirke, Tetsu Yamauchi, and Rabbit Bundrick and cut an LP.)

(b) Wild Turkey. The bassist changed brands in 1970, making two Wild Turkey albums.

(c) Widowmaker. Ex–Spooky Tooth guitarist Luther Grosvenor (who had adopted the name Ariel Bender when he joined Mott the Hoople) and four other Brit-rock veterans put this not-quite-super group together in 1975.

(d) Badger. The original Yes keyboardist bowed out after three LPs and spent a couple of years leading this quartet, unveiled on a 1973 live album.

(e) Magazine. After one EP, the Buzzcocks co-founder left to form the longer-lasting Magazine.

[10 POINTS]

227. 16. Bryan Ferry made five, Brian Eno seven; saxophonist Andy Mackay and guitarist Phil Manzanera each did a pair.

A LABEL OF MY OWN

[1 POINT PER CORRECT ANSWER]

228. (a) Led Zeppelin. The roster included Led Zep, Bad Company, Pretty Things, and Detective.

(b) Elton John. Elton was never on Rocket, but Kiki Dee and Neil Sedaka were.

(c) Ray Davies/Kinks. No Kinks on Konk until the '80s; Claire Hamill and Tom Robinson's pre-TRB band Café Society were the label's big (er . . .) acts in the '70s.

(d) George Harrison. Dark Horse could claim its owner and such lesser-known artistes as Splinter.

(e) Bob Marley and the Wailers. The label was set up in Jamaica in 1971, but the group signed to Island, and Tuff Gong remained a small operation in the overall Wailers picture. In the early '90s, Marley's records were reissued on Tuff Gong.

(f) ELP. The diverse Manticore roster included the Italian group Premiata Forneria Marconi, King Crimson lyricist Pete Sinfield, and British rock trio Stray Dog.

(g) Jefferson Airplane. Besides the Airplane, Grunt released records by the band's extended family: Hot Tuna, Papa John Creach, Peter Kaukonen, et al.

(h) Isaac Hayes. The label was Hayes's custom imprint at ABC Records.

(i) Specials. 2 Tone sparked the British 2 Tone revival with records by Specials, Madness, Selecter, and the Beat.

(j) Barry White. For a time, all White's many recorded enterprises were issued on his own label.

NAMES AND TITLES

[2 POINTS PER CORRECT ANSWER]

229. (a) "Dream On." Aerosmith dreamed the title up first; Sweet put theirs on 1978's

Level Headed.

(b) "I Saw the Light." Both Todd and the 'Berries put original songs with this title on their respective 1972 albums (Something/Anything? and Raspberries); Rundgren got the Top 20 hit.

(c) "It's Too Late." Carole King predated Derek and the Dominos, but the song they recorded was written by Chuck Willis in the late '50s.

(d) "I Want You." Many others have also done songs with this title. Marvin Gaye's was on the LP of the same name; Kiss's was on Rock and Roll Over.

(e) "Love Song." Hard to tell these two songs apart. . .

(f) "Street Life." Roxy Music had a 1973 British hit with it; Neil Diamond sang his song on the 1976 Beautiful Noise LP.

(g) "Surrender." The white flag, from disco (Geils's Monkey Island, 1977) to power pop (Cheap Trick's Heaven Tonight, 1978).

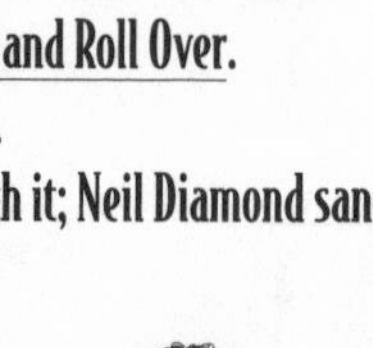

(h) "Take Me I'm Yours." Cheap Trick salvaged a 1977 outtake by this name for their Found All the Parts EP; Squeeze used the same title for a song on their 1978 debut album.

(i) "The Wizard." Black Sabbath and T. Rex—now there's a double bill—each had a song by this name on their respective (1970 and 1971) debuts.

(j) "You and I." This was the title of a 1978 hit single by Rick James and a 1976 album track (A Day at the Races) by Queen.

[2 POINTS PER CORRECT ANSWER]

230. (a) Sparks
(b) Slade
(c) Ultravox
(d) Black Sabbath
(e) Joy Division

[2 POINTS PER CORRECT ANSWER]

231. (a) John Fogerty. The Creedence leader's first solo album was a mostly acoustic collection of country covers, The Blue Ridge Rangers. Although he accepts credit for arranging and producing, Fogerty's name is otherwise not mentioned on the cover.

(b) Colin Blunstone. In 1969, the Zombies vocalist had a British hit—with a remake of the by-then-defunct Zombies' "She's Not There"—under this assumed name.

(c) Wings. Suzy and the Red Stripes was the name on the Top 60 1979 single "Seaside Woman," featuring the songwriting and singing talents of Linda McCartney.

(d) Stranglers. Billed together as Celia and the Mutations, the Stranglers backed an unidentified British singer on a pair of 1977 singles, including a heavy cover of "Mony Mony."

(e) Leon Russell. To be truthful, Hank Wilson isn't exactly a pseudonym—it's Leon Russell's real name. But on Hank Wilson's Back Vol. I, a 1973 album of country and folk standards, the only mention of Leon Russell is as one of four co-producers.

PLAYERS CLUB

[10 POINTS PER CORRECT ANSWER]

232. Lead-singing drummers: respectively, Levon Helm, Kevin Godley, Don Henley, Karen Carpenter, and Phil Seymour.

233. Female bassists. Jackie Fox/Vicki Blue, Sara Lee, Tina Weymouth, Gaye Advert.

234. Three guitarists (at a time).

235. Double drummers (at least onstage).

236. Southpaws. Elliot Easton, Paul McCartney, Jerry Casale, Huw Gower, and Dave Wakeling all play left-handed.

WE BELONG TOGETHER

[10 POINTS PER CORRECT ANSWER]

237. Onetime rock journalists.

238. Titles of 1970s albums by the Ohio Players.

239. Glam bands of the Nicky Chinn/Mike Chapman writing-production stable.

240. Words used more than five times on Born to Run. The most commonly used are "night" (38 appearances) and "street" (18).

241. Roxy Music bassists.

242. Albums that originally had die-cut covers. The Who and Zeppelin records had punchouts that revealed a second layer of art; the Traffic and Horslips record jackets weren't even square.

243. The first artists to release albums on the Virgin Records label after it opened for business in Britain in 1973.

THOSE WACKY BRITS

[1 POINT PER CORRECT ANSWER]

244. (a) Pink Floyd
(b) Lindisfarne
(c) Roxy Music
(d) Slade
(e) Mike Oldfield
(f) Status Quo
(g) Bay City Rollers
(h) Dr. Feelgood
(i) Boney M
(j) Tubeway Army

LOOSE LIPS

[10 POINTS PER CORRECT ANSWER; 5 POINTS FOR EACH PART OF #246]

245. The Clash. The late Lester Bangs asked this question in the early pages of a monumental three-part story he wrote about the Clash for the New Musical Express, later anthologized in Psychotic Reactions and Carburetor Dung.

246. Todd Rundgren; Something/Anything?

247. Boston Phoenix. What he said was, "I saw rock & roll future and its name is Bruce Springsteen."

248. Derf Scratch of Fear. The bassist's remark is followed, logically enough, by guitarist Philo Cramer wondering aloud, "What does 'eat my fuck' mean?" and singer/actor Lee Ving's cogent rejoinder to the linguistic history being made right there onstage: "Fuck you."

249. Bonnie Bramlett. Her reply was reportedly delivered with enough force to knock Elvis on his ass.

250. Johnny Rotten. The comment, made to no one in particular at the end of the band's last-ever gig in San Francisco, is clearly audible in D.O.A., Lech Kowalski's film documentary of the tour.